T0012815

THE

Surprising Return of the Neighborhood Church

Discover How Your Church
Is Primed to Reach Your Neighbors

Sam Rainer

THOM S. RAINER, SERIES EDITOR

A Tyndale nonfiction imprint

Library of Congress Cataloging-in-Publication Data

A catalog record for this book is available from the Library of Congress.

ISBN 987-1-4964-6706-5

Printed in the United States of America

29	28	27	26	25	24	23
7	6	5	4	3	2	1

To the members of West Bradenton.
You believed God would work in the neighborhood,
and he did.

Contents

Calling for a Comeback

"THERE'S A CHURCH ON EVERY CORNER in that community!"

I've heard this comment many times over the years. In most cases, the tone indicates a level of disdain. It's understandable. Church buildings seem to be everywhere, while God's mission seems to be nowhere. But I don't believe we need to give up on these churches. God hasn't.

Your church is located right where God wants it. The problem is that many churches are not doing what God has called them to do where he has placed them. Every church *in* a community exists *for* the community. Your church is God's instrument to reach the neighbors in *your* community.

God doesn't need a plot of land to plant a church, but every spot with a church building has a sovereign strategy from God. Drive around your community and check out each street corner that has a church. At some point in the past, God selected that very spot for his Kingdom work. Maybe the church is already doing great things in the community. Maybe they've struggled for decades. Whatever the case, God doesn't want his work to stop. Until Christ returns, every church is meant to continue God's mission on earth. The life cycle of a church should not include death.

Each location with a church—no matter the size or health of the congregation—is a strategic Kingdom outpost with specific orders from God. What if a movement sprang up in which many of these churches revved back to life and activated their people for service to the Kingdom? I believe we are on the cusp of such a movement. Neighborhood churches experienced a boom following World War II as congregations followed the path of suburban sprawl. Many later faltered and remained dormant for decades. But they are primed for a comeback. Neighborhoods are returning to life as Millennials have families and purchase homes, with many people now working from home. As neighborhoods are revitalizing, the church can make a comeback as well. It's already happening in many places.

Southpoint Fellowship appeared on the precipice of closure for decades. Year after year, the church remained in a state of unhealthy equilibrium, with weekly attendance holding steady at around thirty while a string of bi-vocational pastors came and went. Just enough giving came through to pay the bills. The piano player faithfully showed up every week for worship. The same group of people gathered every Sunday, enjoyed their fellowship, and then went home.

The church members cared for each other. There were meal trains and prayer meetings. About once a year, a new couple would join the church, bringing just enough growth to offset the loss of those who moved away or died. Eventually and inevitably, however, the church of fiftysomethings and sixtysomethings became a church of eightysomethings, and members started passing away at a rate that outpaced the arrival of new people. Soon, Southpoint had declined to about twenty people; and a short time later, they were down to about a dozen regulars. The weekly offering started to dip, and the piano player could no longer drive to church on her own. Then the latest bi-vocational pastor moved to another town and could no longer commute to preach.

One long-standing member refused to give up. She reached out to another local pastor for help.

"We don't want our church to die. What should we do?"

"How many of you live in the neighborhood?" the pastor asked.

"We all moved to other places about fifteen years ago, and we drive in each Sunday."

The pastor knew it would be a challenge to help this struggling church, but he felt compelled to do something. Southpoint was the only church in that particular neighborhood. The coastal community was changing quickly as affluent, young Hispanic families moved in and elderly homeowners on fixed incomes sold their homes and moved out. A major apartment development had just been completed one block away from the church. And a new police station was being built across the street. God's Kingdom could use this prime, two-acre location in the heart of a transitioning neighborhood.

"We can help you," said the pastor, "but I have no idea what God might do here."

"Anything God does will be better than what we've done the last twenty years."

The following week, the pastor received a call from a friend in ministry.

"We've got a young, bilingual intern looking to become a pastor. He's moving to your community, and we're willing to fund his ministry for three years. Do you have a place for him?"

Two years later, the church of a dozen members had grown to an average attendance of about sixty, and they had a children's ministry for the first time since the 1980s. The neighborhood was abuzz about the ministry there, and the police officers especially enjoyed the baked goods that church members brought to the station each week.

The Southpoint turnaround is remarkable, but it shouldn't be unusual. Chances are there's a church strategically located near you that is poised for a similar move of God. Neighborhood churches everywhere can grow from a small group of survivors to a thriving body of Kingdom workers. The neighborhood church is about to make a surprising return, but it will not happen automatically.

How can your church and other churches in your community seize the opportunity?

The Opportunity Is Right Down the Road

The importance of neighborhood churches is underscored by the findings of a 2017 Baylor University study that 68 percent of church attendees live within fifteen minutes of the church they attend, and 21 percent live five minutes or less from their place of worship. Only 9 percent live more than half an hour from their church.[1] The setting of the church—urban, suburban, or rural—has no bearing on people's willingness to commute. What was fascinating, however, was the influence that churches have on neighborhood satisfaction. Even adjusting for "religious tradition and location size," the study found that "the people most satisfied with their neighborhood are those who attend congregations in the neighborhood."[2] It's a hopeful sign for neighborhood churches.

In the not-so-distant past, growing churches often relocated away from their neighborhoods and built large campuses at major intersections. The thought was that the drive would be worth the distance. This strategy seemed to work when these large churches were master-planning their sprawling campuses in the 1970s to early 2000s. They were championed and celebrated. Many large churches grew at tremendous rates, and many of them accomplished an incredible amount of good for the Kingdom of God, continuing even today.

But starting around the turn of the twenty-first century, many of the largest churches shifted to multisite campuses and multiple venues. The massive, single-site church was no longer the focus of their planning. A glance at the Outreach 100 list of largest churches reveals that almost all of them have grown through multiple site expansion since 2000.[3]

Something further changed around 2010, when the exponential growth in the number of US megachurches slowed, and then all but stopped, prior to the pandemic.[4] How will the pandemic affect the number of megachurches? The answer will take years to uncover, but I believe it's a safe assumption that the largest churches haven't benefited from the events of 2020 and 2021.

In the Neighborhood but Not Ready for the Neighbors

What does a neighborhood church look like? How is a neighborhood church different from other kinds of churches? I will answer these questions in depth in chapter 1, but for now let's look at the definition of a neighborhood church.

In the simplest terms, a neighborhood church is one that is surrounded by residences within the recognized boundaries of a specific neighborhood. Suburban subdivisions can be neighborhoods.

Enclaves within a small town can be neighborhoods. Boroughs of large cities can contain many neighborhoods.

A neighborhood is a local community of residences with a recognized identity, often distinct from other surrounding areas. Neighborhoods are both geographic and social. For example, sometimes a city council or other government agency will define exact boundaries of a neighborhood, but people may identify with a neighborhood even if they live outside the established boundaries. A neighborhood is a *place*, but also a *social attachment*.

Neighborhood churches are congregations located geographically in and socially identified with a particular neighborhood. The name of the neighborhood might even be reflected in the name of the church. My childhood church, Azalea Baptist in St. Petersburg, Florida, is surrounded by homes, with the Azalea Community Garden next door and Azalea Middle School across the street.

Neighborhood churches are typically small to midsize established congregations. A church may be planted with the vision of becoming a neighborhood church, but it may take years to be accepted as such. A well-established presence at a particular address is key to becoming a neighborhood church.

Most importantly, neighborhood churches are culturally woven into the fabric of the local community. A neighborhood church exists not only *in* the community but also *for* the community.[5] Neighborhood churches are in every city and small town across the United States. Though it's difficult to get an exact count, they are perhaps the largest single category of churches. Neighborhood churches are numerous, and it's time to leverage those numbers into a movement of revitalization and renewed health.

But here's the problem. The typical neighborhood church isn't prepared for an influx of new people. They aren't primed for growth. Though they are in their neighborhoods geographically, they are not fully present culturally or missiologically. They are not geared to understand or reach their changing neighborhoods. Most American churches are small—with fewer than one hundred people. Most American churches have been in existence for decades.[6] Though there are far more small and midsize churches than megachurches, the trend toward larger churches has been in place for many years. The largest one percent of Protestant churches, for example, comprise approximately 15 percent of all the people, money, and staff.[7] Small neighborhood churches are used to being small and often do not think about growth beyond their current size.

As the megachurch movement has begun to wane, it presents an opportunity for smaller and midsize established churches. The problem is that people won't flock back into neighborhood churches from larger churches simply because it's a shorter drive from home. Most churches—of all sizes—are smaller than they were a few years ago, due to the pandemic. The revitalization of neighborhood churches is not a foregone conclusion. It will take a lot of work, but I believe it can happen. Many neighborhood churches are right around the corner but off the radar. Your neighborhood church can regain the attention of the neighbors. The potential for this movement is enormous. I believe you can be a part of it.

The Potential Neighborhood Church Movement

When I see a church on three acres buried in a dense neighborhood, I don't think "landlocked and limited potential." I see opportunity. Who else is better situated to reach the people there? These little churches that dot the landscape of many cities, towns, and suburbs may be in desperate need of revitalization, but they have a future. I don't believe that God intends to give up these strategic corners of the Kingdom. There is significant hope for neighborhood churches across North America because many church leaders and their congregations are leveraging their resources and reclaiming their neighborhoods for Christ.

My aim here is to help you realize the tremendous potential of the neighborhood church. We need to get excited about how God can use these congregations that are already situated in neighborhoods across our nation. A church on every street corner is precisely how God's Kingdom can grow!

Chapter 1 examines the mission of neighborhood churches and how so many have declined over the last several decades. The Great Commission and the Great Commandment apply to every church globally, but neighborhood churches have a distinct calling to weave into the fabric of their communities. Your church address is not an accident. God has sovereignly selected each location, and every church has a responsibility to serve and reach the people who live nearby.

Chapter 2 points to the bright future of neighborhood churches. Although they grew quickly in the 1950s and 1960s, following the path of suburban sprawl, many of these churches eventually became destination points *from* the neighborhood rather than reaching people *within* the neighborhood. This chapter addresses both the history of the neighborhood church and emerging opportunities.

Chapter 3 reveals the marks of a healthy neighborhood church—starting with how they create ministries uniquely tailored to the immediate community. Neighborhood church leaders should be connected to the community power grid and recognize their potential for impact. Healthy neighborhood churches view their community as a place to *serve*, not as a pool of people to merely add to the membership rolls.

Chapter 4 explores a new framework for neighborhood churches. The perspective of the community and the perspective of the church are jointly utilized in this framework. Understanding both perspectives is critical to leading a neighborhood church back to health.

Chapter 5 debunks some myths about neighborhood churches. Too many church leaders assume that neighborhood churches have a limited potential for impact. The problems are real but not insurmountable. A landlocked campus is just as much an asset as it is a limitation. And a small congregation doesn't necessarily mean a small influence. Neighborhood churches are more than just a vestige of a previous, older generation. It's time to push through these myths and capture the true potential of the neighborhood church.

Chapter 6 unpacks what needs to change in order for neighborhood churches to fulfill their potential. Growth and influence will not occur automatically. It will take work to overcome the various challenges. If a large number of neighborhood churches were already healthy and growing, the movement would be at full steam. The reason it's not is mainly because too many neighborhood churches are unhealthy. Most neighborhood churches must *change* in order to become a vital presence in their community.

Chapter 7 evaluates how to lead change in a neighborhood church. *Trust* is more important than *vision*. The church must get out of the *power run* cycle—whether it is run by the pastor, one or more families, or a group of influencers. The pace must be accelerated while not derailing the change effort. This chapter also looks at several cultural issues within neighborhood church congregations. Is the church healthy and willing? Or is it entrenched, desperate, or on life support?

Chapter 8 demonstrates effective ways to reach the neighbors. There is hope for leaders and members of neighborhood churches!

I share specific and concrete ways congregations can reach their neighborhoods. Many paths are available immediately, and they can be accomplished even with minimal financial resources. These ideas can move neighborhood churches from scapegoat excuses to positive action right now.

Chapter 9 discusses how to become a neighborhood church for the nations. The global mandate to reach every tongue, tribe, and nation cannot be neglected, even when a neighborhood church is going through the process of revitalizing their local mission. All neighborhood churches must have a corresponding heart for the nations. Without this global perspective, many neighborhood churches will stop moving outward and revert to an inward perspective.

The conclusion looks at what you can do to make the neighborhood church comeback a reality. These unnoticed and often neglected churches are about to fire back to life. If we can get them moving, then a major Kingdom advance is ready to happen.

Some pastors in established churches don't know how good they have it. There are church planters out there setting up and tearing down every week in movie theaters and schools. Sure, your roof leaks. I get how frustrating it can be. In my church, I inherited an old, tiny one-seater bathroom on the main hallway. The light switch also turned on a fan, which swirled so loudly that the first time I went in there, I thought the rapture was occurring. But we have a permanent location and an address everyone knows. Our real estate is a huge benefit to our ministry. The opportunity is one of geography, demographics, and sociology. But there is a greater reason to be excited about the neighborhood church. Spiritually, these churches can reach neighborhoods across the United States for Christ. God's mission awaits. Let's go reach our neighbors!

1

Your Address Is Your Assignment

EVERY LOCAL CHURCH has a clear assignment given directly by God. Your address is your assignment. The location of your church is God's strategy to reach and serve the community. No church is called to *sit*. All churches are *sent*. The church is not a destination. The church is a vehicle designed by God to take the good news of Jesus into our neighborhoods.

As I mentioned in the introduction, I spent my childhood in St. Petersburg, Florida. We lived on 28th Avenue North, and our church, Azalea Baptist, was located on 22nd Avenue North. Because my father was the pastor, I spent many weekdays roaming the church and the neighborhood. One of the members was a pipe organ specialist who traveled the world in his job. In his spare time, he built one for Azalea. One of my favorite hideaway spots was the organ area, with its many pipes, sounds, and secrets.

Recently, two leaders from Azalea contacted me. The church had declined to about twenty people. It's a familiar story, but one that shook me. I remember the days of a lively sanctuary, lots of children, and my father busy with a growing congregation. My surprise was not that a church in St. Petersburg was in decline. The area has become a wasteland for churches, with many closing and selling off their property—about two each month. Once thriving campuses are now home to an insurance company, a fast-food restaurant, and several residential developments.

One church with an average age of seventy-four received an investor's offer to buy their church property. At first they considered it "a nudge from the Lord," but they made the right decision to continue ministry in their location.

"We are reinvesting," the pastor said. "We are more cohesive in understanding what our financial situation is, what our membership demographics are, what our challenges are. Now time is ticking. We have to do something."[1]

The time is short for Azalea, as well. I met with the current leadership, and they pulled out an old photo album with pictures from the 1980s and early 1990s. My family was on almost every page. Tears welled in my eyes. My childhood was the church's heyday. Unfortunately, an album did not exist for the last several years, because there was not much of a story to tell.

"We want to be like this again," one longtime member said, pointing to the album.

"Then you can't be like you are now," I replied.

The Message, the Messenger, and the Mission

Three "greats" stand out in the Gospels: the Great Confession (Matthew 16:13-20; Mark 8:27-30), where Peter declares Jesus as the Messiah; the Great Commandment (Matthew 22:34-40; Luke

10:25-37), that we are to love God and love our neighbors; and the Great Commission (Matthew 28:16-20), to make disciples of all nations. The Great Confession reveals the message: *Jesus saves*. The Great Commandment clarifies the posture of the messenger: *love*. And the Great Commission demonstrates the mission: *making disciples*. The key to each of these three greats is the outward movement of God and his people.

God's work in the world involves *sending*. Francis DuBose, in his classic missiological work, *God Who Sends*, calls this "the divine modus operandi"—that is, God's method of operation.[2] God works through outward movement. His *message* (Great Confession) must be proclaimed by *messengers* (Great Commandment) sent on a *mission* (Great Commission) to share good news. Though the implications of this biblical principle are profound, one lesson is obvious: A stagnant, stationary church is a disobedient church; whereas a church on the move is following God's design. DuBose rightly notes that humanity is both the *object* and *instrument* of God's sending. God desires to have a personal relationship with humanity (object), and this desire is communicated through other people (instrument).

Jesus clearly instructed us to love our neighbors. Love is an active decision, not merely an emotion. Too many relationships fall apart because they are based on how people feel. Frankly, the foundation of biblical love is actions, not feelings. If we do the actions of love, the feelings of love will follow. When we love our husband or wife, our parents or children, through right actions, they will feel loved. The same goes for our neighbors. If we show them the actions of love, they will feel loved. If we are struggling to love our neighbors, we can do the acts of love, and our emotions of love will follow. Love is proven by what we *do*. It is not based on how we may feel at any given moment.

The people of the church are both messengers and neighbors. As messengers, we deliver God's truth. Every believer is an ambassador for Jesus. An ambassador is a person sent to a foreign place to speak and act on behalf of his or her government. The ambassador is a country's highest-ranking representative to other nations. Though their day-to-day responsibilities will differ based on their assignment, all ambassadors are responsible to represent the best interests of the sending nation.

We are ambassadors for our King, Jesus, and we represent the interests of God's Kingdom. We are sent to proclaim the message of truth—the good news about Jesus. This truth is not to be modified. The gospel doesn't need improvement. The message of truth is not to be restrained or watered down. The gospel message is good news to all humanity, just as Jesus himself is good news.

While we must share the message about Jesus without compromising the truth, we must deliver this good news with love. As Paul writes in Ephesians 4:15, the way that we grow to become "more and more like Christ" is to "speak the truth in love." We bring God's truth as *messengers*, and we do so in a spirit of love as *neighbors*. In Matthew 22:39, Jesus explicitly commands us to love our neighbors. But a similar account in Luke 10 raises an important question: Who is our neighbor? Is God's good news for everyone? Are his messengers obligated to bring the message to *every* neighbor?

I've had some strange neighbors. Maybe you can relate. One in particular is unforgettable. He would stand in his yard over a bonfire with nothing on but a bathrobe, smoking pot for hours. He fueled the fire with fallen branches from trees in the neighborhood. (In that way, he helped keep our yards clean.) My wife and I simply called him Bathrobe Guy. One time Erin made him cookies, but he may have been disappointed they weren't "fortified." We invited him to church, half wondering whether he might take us up on "come as you are."

Bathrobe Guy needs Jesus. Your neighbors need Jesus—and, yes, that includes the corner curmudgeon, the loud car dude, and the yippy dog lady. All our neighbors need to hear the message of Jesus from us. People who do not act like us, look like us, or have the same interests we do are exactly the people God wants us to reach.

Jesus told a parable to make the point that everyone is our neighbor—even the most unlikely people. In Luke 10:25-42, an expert in the law challenged Jesus, hoping to trap him with a trick question. This expert stood up to ask the question, an outward sign of respect and honor. But the intent of his question was to "test Jesus," which reveals an inward attitude problem.

The expert asked Jesus which law was the greatest. In typical rabbinic style, Jesus answered the question with another question: "What does the law of Moses say?" The answer was one the legal expert knew well: "You must love the LORD your God with all your heart, all your soul, all your strength, and all your mind. And, 'love your neighbor as yourself.'"

Jesus' rejoinder was perfect: "Right!"

The expert then tried to justify himself, asking, "And who is my neighbor?"

He probably expected Jesus to say something to the effect of "your friends, your coworkers, and people you like." But Jesus cut to the core with one of the most recognizable parables in the New Testament, the story of the Good Samaritan, which established a foundational biblical truth: *Everyone is your neighbor.*

Martin Luther King, Jr. offered a remarkable insight into this parable: "I can imagine that the first question which the Priest and the Levite asked was: 'If I stop to help this man, what will happen to me?' Then the Good Samaritan came by, and by the very nature of his concern reversed the question: 'If I do not stop to help this man, what will happen to him?'"[3]

Why serve the homeless? Why foster a child? Why befriend someone of a different political persuasion? Because of what Jesus teaches in this parable. When it involves the message of Jesus, it's not our place to limit who hears it. If we believe that God can save *anyone*, we should be willing to share the gospel with *everyone*.

We also cannot specify *when* we will share. The Great Commandment is not based on our convenience. Have you ever noticed that serving others is rarely convenient? Like the priest and Levite in the parable, we can come up with a variety of legitimate excuses to avoid serving our neighbors.

Sharing God's truth in love comes with a level of risk. We could be hurt emotionally. In some places in the world, there is a chance of being hurt physically. People might take advantage of us. Or they may laugh us off. But we mustn't forget that at one time we were that person on the side of the road, beaten and dying. And Jesus was the one who stopped to save us. Jesus is the Good Samaritan—the perfect neighbor.

As sent ambassadors, carriers of the message of Jesus, we have a job to do. But our job is not to recruit our neighbors to come to church. Rather, we are to invite them to become part of the most extraordinary mission the world has ever known—the proclamation of the glory of God to the ends of the earth. Why do we exist? Our lives matter to the extent that our mission is to bring glory to God. In Isaiah 43:5-7, the prophet proclaims that God will gather his children from all over the world, even "from the distant corners of the earth." Why? God tells us: "I have made them for my glory." We were made to be saved. Saved to be sent. And sent for the glory of God.

The Unique Features of a Neighborhood Church

God's mission travels in one vehicle: the church. As David Platt has written, "We are the plan of God, and there is no plan B."[4] In the same way that different kinds of vehicles travel our roadways, many different churches share the good news message. The neighborhood church is but one kind of church. No congregation has a corner on the Kingdom, and every Bible-believing church has the potential to be an asset in the Kingdom of God. But the unique characteristics of a neighborhood church make it a powerful tool to reach local communities.

What exactly defines a neighborhood church? How are neighborhood churches different from other kinds of churches?

Surrounded by Residences

One of the easiest ways to spot a neighborhood church is that its campus will be bordered by residences. These churches are not located on major thoroughfares or at exits on the interstate. Many were planted at the same time the neighborhood formed, without any consideration of drawing people from other parts of town. Often, neighborhood churches are built just before an area becomes populated and homes go up around the church. People in the neighborhood know the location of these churches, but those who live outside the neighborhood may not know they exist.

Centrally Located

Neighborhood churches are located at the heart of a social network. They are near public parks and schools. In some communities, they are just around the corner from a main commercial area. Anyone in the community can quickly drive to the church, and many will be within walking distance. The parking lot of a neighborhood church is where children learn to ride their bikes.

The church playground is utilized by young families, even if they don't attend. People who enjoy walking may swing by the church campus, and those with dogs will conveniently forget to clean up messes in the grass.

Built into the Fabric of the Community

When the local elementary school is looking for sponsors, the neighborhood church is often included in the mix with commercial businesses. You may see the church logo on the outfield fence at Little League games. Graduation ceremonies are held in the sanctuary. Though geography obviously locates the church within the neighborhood, it is the social connections that solidify the church's identity as part of the community. A healthy neighborhood church will have members who are schoolteachers, local business owners, and service workers. One of the defining features of a neighborhood church is how the members are embedded in the cultural context of the neighborhood.[5] Neighborhood churches are connected to the local culture, often at a micro level. The influence of these churches is limited to a few blocks in an urban area or a couple square miles in a suburban or rural area. Though restricted by geography, the cultural impact of a neighborhood church can be substantial among the people who live nearby.

Established History and Legacy

Most neighborhood churches have long-standing locations and extensive histories within the community. Sometimes these histories are recorded and documented as part of the local folklore. The reputation of a neighborhood church can be both positive and negative. Indeed, most have a mixed bag of successes and failures throughout their histories. Their legacies are rarely pristine. And it is common for generations of families to be connected to the neighborhood church, even if some family members no longer attend.

Capped Size and Footprint

Though neighborhood churches can be quite large, with upwards of a thousand in attendance on a weekly basis, most are much smaller. Neighborhood church campuses tend to have landlocked lots and limited parking. Sites of two to four acres are common. The limitations on attendance and facilities are typical but shouldn't be disconcerting. No church can grow infinitely. Though most neighborhood churches are in need of revitalization and increased attendance, the goal is not to become megachurches. Indeed, the physical limitations of the campus often act as a natural ceiling on membership size. Still, there is a bright future for neighborhood churches and their bounded campuses. But first we must determine how so many neighborhood churches lost their sense of mission and fell into decline.

Why Neighborhood Churches Decline

No doubt you've heard the phrase, "There goes the neighborhood." Historically, it has been associated with ethnic minorities moving into white neighborhoods.[6] Tensions reached a fever pitch during the era of desegregation, and to some degree they are still present today. During the civil rights movement and the following decades, many white neighborhood churches changed locations, often moving to the growing suburbs where fewer minorities lived. For the congregations that stayed, the fracturing of the neighborhood also meant the fracturing of the church. Many neighborhood churches struggled to understand the changing demographics and failed to reach their new neighbors. Once the ties were cut in these communities that had bound the people into a single, comprehensive village, many churches struggled to find their place in what they viewed as a fragmented world.[7] The mission of every church is to go into a fragmented world and share the good news of Jesus that heals the brokenness. Historically, many neighborhood churches believed their meaning and identity would shift with changing demographics. Such thinking was antithetical to the gospel. The white flight of churches was horrid, but it alone does not explain the decline of neighborhood churches. More was at play and is still affecting these churches today.

A Me-First Mentality

Inward-focused churches always decline. Some more quickly than others. But spiritual navel-gazing always kills a church. People with a me-first mentality believe the church exists to meet their needs rather than as a way for them to serve their community. When personal preferences are elevated above God's mission, the church will turn inward, creating a culture of selfishness and entitlement. The operating budget is often the first indication of inward movement, even before attendance begins to decline. When money that once was allocated for outreach evangelism shifts to ministries that serve the members, the church is moving inward.

During the pandemic, a pastor in the upper Midwest shared his frustration with me. Over the past decade, his church had declined from almost two hundred in attendance to less than fifty.

"Before all this, they were fighting about the color of paint on the walls. They are *still* fighting about the paint. The only difference is that now they are yelling at each other through masks."

The me-first mentality can pertain to trivial matters such as the color of the paint or the carpet, or to more consequential issues such as ethnic minorities moving into the neighborhood. The result, however, is inevitably the same: An inward culture will always kill a neighborhood church.

Church Bubble Syndrome

"I'm interested in joining your church, but I'm struggling with all the foster children here. They can be rowdy, and I don't know if I want my children around them."

Though I understood this mother's concern, I had to inform her that our church was not a bubble to shield its members from the community. Instead, we had a specific calling as a neighborhood church to help tackle the toughest issues in the community. Sadly, she chose not to join our church.

When a church views its role as protecting members from the rough-and-tumble world of the surrounding community, walls will inevitably go up. Though these walls aren't physical, they might as well be—letting certain people know they're not welcome. And when you stop welcoming one kind of person, it becomes much easier to stop welcoming others, as well. Some neighborhood churches declined because they tried to exist for only part of the neighborhood. Ironically, most would probably say, "All are welcome!" I've even seen that phrase on church signs. But it doesn't take long to figure out who is truly welcome and who is not. Church bubble syndrome limits the reach of the gospel into the surrounding community, and God will not honor churches that limit his mission.

No Expectation of Growth

I mentioned that no church can grow indefinitely. Even massive churches with exponential growth curves will eventually slow down. It's a physical reality due to the size of their campuses. It's also a statistical and sociological reality. But far too few neighborhood churches have a culture and expectation of growth. There was a palpable excitement in these large congregations during the heyday of megachurch growth in the 1990s and early 2000s. Their people expected and wanted growth.

If you examine a neighborhood church in decline, you will often find a congregation with an entrenched mentality. They want the church to stay the way it is. Visitors are welcome so long as there aren't too many at once. Growth is viewed as a risk, and new people become a threat to the ideal size of the church.

Unnoticed Demographic Mismatches

In a recent consultation with a neighborhood church, I asked the leaders what percentage of their community was ethnic minorities. Their responses varied from about 5 percent to 15 percent. When I showed them the actual statistics, they were shocked. About 45 percent of the community was African American or Hispanic.

Then I asked them which generation was the largest in their community. Every leader said Baby Boomers, though in fact the Boomers were fourth, behind the Gen Xers, Millennials, and Generation Z. They had a hard time believing me.

"Where do you go? Who do you hang out with?" I asked.

They all admitted their worlds were quite small, even within the neighborhood. They hung out at the same places and with the same people. These church leaders had not noticed the demographic change in their community because they unintentionally avoided it. Though they were not opposed to reaching a new segment of people, their patterns of living and inward-focused church culture kept them from seeing the reality that was right in front of them.

Lack of Vibrant Prayer

Most churches pray. Just about any church of any size, background, or doctrinal persuasion will pray. But are they perfunctory prayers or vibrant prayers? For example, we have a deacon in our church named Daryll, and I love to hear him pray because you can tell he genuinely believes God will work. Though he is soft-spoken, he urges God to move. He's passionate and emotionally engaged.

Does your church pray more for hip surgeries than for gospel conversations? Both are important, but you should place more emphasis on God seeking the lost. Of course, Jesus heals physically, and we should ask God for such healing. But Jesus didn't say of his mission, "For the Son of Man came to seek and save those having surgeries." A vibrant prayer life in the church will be weighted toward pleading with God to save your lost neighbors.

One of the first books on revitalizing neighborhood churches, *Basic Communities: A Practical Guide for Renewing Neighborhood Churches* by Thomas Maney, was written in 1984. It was way ahead of its time. Maney correctly identifies prayer as the key to neighborhood church renewal. He notes that prayer prompts a congregation to move from indifference to enthusiasm, from being bored to being engaged.[8] Neighborhood churches in decline almost always lack vibrant prayer.

Poor Leadership Coupled with Apathy or Antagonism toward the Community

I don't know of a neighborhood church that relies on the personality of a nationally known leader with charisma. Growth or decline in these churches is based on issues at the local level and not the global platform of their pastors. But every church requires leadership. The most influential leader is typically the lead or sole pastor—the one preaching during worship services.

When leaders respond poorly to the surrounding culture, the church will tend toward one of two responses: *apathy* or *antagonism*. Some pastors even encourage these responses through poor leadership. A church that doesn't work to understand or listen to the community culture will inevitably stop caring for the neighborhood or will start hating the people there. Apathetic churches become islands and disengage from the neighborhood. Nothing may physically change about the campus, yet the church will mysteriously slip into oblivion in the minds of the community.

While an apathetic church may go completely unnoticed, an antagonistic church will garner much attention. Lawsuits against the local government, negative campaigns against school boards, protests against local businesses, and extreme measures such as book burnings are all tactics of antagonistic neighborhood churches.

The community knows nothing about the apathetic church, while the antagonistic church is known for what they oppose. A healthy neighborhood church will be known for what it supports, and it will have leaders who respond graciously to changes in the local culture.

Unattractive Facilities

Some neighborhood churches seem to care very little for their campuses. They've gained a reputation as eyesores rather than points of pride in the community. Too many neighborhood churches are not investing in their God-given addresses. A church campus should be the most well-kept spot in the neighborhood. Why would someone visit a church when the campus looks more like a run-down gas station than a place where people worship Almighty God? If the members don't care about their facility, how will they care for their neighbors?

Conversely, there are neighborhood churches that care more for their campus than they do for the surrounding community. They put up locks and chains and don't allow any outside use of their facilities. A run-down campus is unattractive because it is an eyesore, but an inaccessible campus is unattractive because it tells the neighbors they're not welcome.

A Shift to a Brighter Future

Neighborhood churches have the potential to be the both nimble and flexible. Typically, they have smaller campuses, which often means less deferred maintenance compared to larger church facilities. And whereas larger regional churches must consider a broader demographic of people from various locations, ministries at neighborhood churches can be tailored specifically to the people right around the church. In the era of waning denominational loyalty, neighborhood churches can capture people based on their local presence rather than denominational preference. Though many challenges remain for neighborhood churches, a vibrant sense of mission is just waiting to be renewed. Your location is a key asset, and the future is bright. Let's turn our attention now to the prospect of a better tomorrow.

2

The (Bright) Future of Neighborhood Churches

WE WALKED PAST MOUNDS of clothing, old silk flower arrangements, and a collection of record and cassette players in the upstairs wing of a neighborhood church. Mice had wreaked havoc over the years. The air conditioning no longer worked. The smell of urine was overwhelming.

"When was the last time the church used this floor?"

"I don't know. Maybe the mid-1980s."

Matt, the pastor who invited us to visit, had inherited a mess. Only twenty people remained in the church when he arrived. The peak had occurred sometime in the 1970s, when attendance topped six hundred. Several buildings on the large campus had been constructed between the 1950s and the 1980s. When the church started declining, the congregation abandoned parts of the campus, one floor or one building at a time. Over decades, the congregation occupied less and less of the campus, and the unused rooms decayed to the point of disrepair.

"I'm bringing in a dumpster this week, and we're getting rid of this stuff."

He picked up a stained purple tablecloth. It was one of dozens in a large pile in the middle of the room.

"They dropped these items in here, locked the door, and left them to rot."

The physical deterioration of the church campus matched the spiritual decline of the congregation. Years of poor pastoral leadership had compounded a sense of apathy among the people. The remnant had all but resigned themselves to their fate when Matt came to the church.

He tried to energize the congregation with a fresh set of initiatives.

"What does it matter?" one older member said at Matt's first business meeting. "We're going to close anyway."

After a few conversations, Matt understood why the church was resigned to defeat. The previous pastor had wanted to close the church and give the building to the denomination. For the last several years, every leadership decision was made through the lens of inevitable closure.

"We're not closing the doors," Matt repeated at every opportunity.

Then the church started talking about how to *open* the doors to the community instead. They attempted a block party. Thirty children and their families came. The church was discouraged by the low turnout, but Matt kept pushing. Their next attempt was a neighborhood Christmas party. Over six hundred people from the community attended.

"I guess I'd forgotten you were here," one neighbor said.

"People can drive by your church every day on their way to work, but you are invisible until you make your presence known through ministry in the neighborhood," Matt remarked as we meandered through the campus.

Gradually, the church began to grow. Then the pandemic took the wind out of their sails, and attendance took a big hit. Like many churches, they closed the doors for a season. But as soon as they were able, they opened up again and rekindled their ministry efforts. Not every event worked, and their renovation of the campus was painfully slow. But the mentality had changed. The culture shifted from expecting closure to expecting guests. Almost one hundred people from the neighborhood now claim the church as their home.

"We have a long way to go," Matt told me, "and I'm not sure what to do with this massive campus. But we're going to make it. There is no other church in this neighborhood. Tens of thousands live around us. If we don't survive, no one will be left to share the gospel here."

The following week, the church started a massive cleaning effort, hauling off truckloads of junk. In a way, the physical cleaning of the campus symbolized a spiritual cleaning—out with the old and in with the new.

The Past, Present, and Future Hope of Neighborhoods

The story of Matt's church expresses a common theme and pattern. A church that started with the development of a new neighborhood. Then the congregation went through a period of decline as the neighborhood regressed. Over a couple of decades, the church campus deteriorated as attendance numbers waned. The neighborhood experienced a rebirth (or is currently in the process of rebirth), but the church didn't experience the same renewal.

Though these churches should have changed course years ago to adapt to their surroundings, they are now waking up to the reality that they may not survive another ten years. The Covid-19 pandemic exacerbated and accelerated whatever problems were already there. We're now at a turning point with many neighborhood churches. Does the future include any hope for them? I believe so. But first, I want to examine the neighborhood dynamics that accompany church declines. We must understand the context of these churches to lead them to a brighter tomorrow.

What Makes a Neighborhood?

A single classification system doesn't exist for determining the boundaries of a neighborhood. Census tracts, resident-perceived boundaries, physical and spatial buffers (e.g., major roads), and activity-mapping where people spend their time are all methods of verifying the parameters of a neighborhood.[1] From a research perspective, understanding what defines a neighborhood is both an objective and a subjective exercise—both an art and a science. Many American neighborhoods coalesced around the ideal of mixing the best of urban density with the best of a countryside setting. The community of a neighborhood is not something one can consume, like a pizza, nor is it something we can buy, like a trip to Disney World. A neighborhood community is a living organism, cared for and loved by its residents, in which everything relates to the others in a way that makes sense.[2] In this book, I will define a neighborhood as a perceived place recognized by residents as their community with a general geography distinct from surrounding areas.

Where Did Neighborhoods Originate?

A few thousand years ago, people formed a new kind of settlement, a permanent association of families and neighbors in which generation after generation lived.[3] The village was a precursor to the concept of a neighborhood. With its protective walls, the ancient city kept power concentrated and invaders out. The medieval town brought people together economically and religiously, often mixing the two—resulting in massive houses of worship. Industrialization prompted more people to leave the countryside and seek a better life in what were the beginnings of the modern city or town. The growth of cities and towns led to the formation of neighborhoods. People created micro-communities as the surrounding area grew. When you visit older cities in Europe or Asia, you can see the progression and expansion of neighborhoods through various eras. The concept of a neighborhood is an old one. Still, the ones we recognize today are the by-products of a desire to escape the polluted and chaotic manufacturing centers of cities that grew during the Industrial Revolution.

Suburban Sprawl and Neighborhood Growth Today

The neighborhoods of the Industrial Revolution were often segregated by socioeconomics. The well-to-do were the only ones who had the means to leave the city. Quieter and cleaner neighborhoods had many obvious benefits, but escapism also created many problems. During this time, Rudyard Kipling wrote to William James about the future issues created by this urban/rural segregation: "Half your trouble is the curse of America—sheer, hopeless, well-ordered boredom; and that is going some day to be the curse of the world."[4] Even in 1896, Kipling recognized the downside of sprawl and segregation. Escaping the city's troubles would only create more problems down the road. Kipling's words were prophetic in many ways.

The critiques of neighborhood and suburban sprawl are numerous. Many are well-warranted. Sprawling expansion can leave behind the elderly and the immobile poor in declining, less desirable parts of cities and towns. Urban cores in areas such as Detroit and St. Louis experienced significant deterioration as people moved into neighborhoods farther removed from the industrialized city center. Often, African American communities suffered as wealthier whites moved to different neighborhoods. Practices like redlining, an illegal and discriminatory practice through which banks did not make loans to Black communities, kept certain neighborhoods of ethnic minorities from creating greater net worth through home ownership. Timothy Keller, in his seminal work titled *Center Church*, notes the theological tension of the city.[5] On the one hand, cities hold much potential for producing positive social reform. On the other hand, they can also be vehicles for enhancing rebellion against God.[6]

In the United States, a boom of neighborhoods occurred after World War II. The most obvious reason was the rise of the Baby Boomer generation. As more families were having more babies, the nation needed more homes to accommodate the population growth. In the 1940s and 1950s, the Federal Housing Administration and Veterans Administration created loan programs to provide mortgages for millions of new homes. They were aimed at new single-family construction in the suburbs.[7] It was cheaper to buy a new home than to rent, and it was easier to buy new than to renovate an older home. Aided by the expanding interstate highway system, people built new neighborhoods in the suburbs and commuted into downtown city centers for work and shopping. But within a couple of decades, many of those places of employment and commerce moved out to the suburbs, where the more affluent people lived, leaving behind a struggling city center. Though the concept of suburban sprawl is often mentioned with a level of disdain, certain aspects of these new neighborhoods point to a better future.

Neighborhoods and suburban sprawl are two concepts inter-twined with each other. Established neighborhoods in most cities and towns are simply the result of suburban sprawl from decades prior. In some places, grid patterns have given way to cul-de-sacs, but the long-standing desire to live between the center of town and the countryside remains. Suburbs are simply newer forms of established neighborhoods. And the dynamics of growth are changing.

The outward migration of the wealthy that occurred in the mid-twentieth century is ending as the Millennial generation begins to settle into existing suburbs, making them more densely populated.[8] Additionally, many urban cores are recovering eco-nomically through gentrification. Almost every region in the United States is expected to increase in population density, not decrease.[9] Contrary to popular beliefs about suburban sprawl, Robert Bruegmann contends that "the suburbs of American cities are, if anything, becoming denser. Suburban lot sizes, after peak-ing in the 1950s, have been declining, and the number of square feet of land used by the average house in new developments at the suburban edge has fallen sharply in the past ten years even as the houses themselves have grown in size."[10] The younger generations are also significantly more ethnically diverse. Wealth is expected to become more of an issue than race. As the Millennials and their children get older, socioeconomics will become the prevailing dividing line instead of racial differences.[11]

What is fueling the rise of denser suburbs? The simple answer is population growth. In 1950, the US population was about 150 million. By 2022, it had more than doubled, to about 335 million. As revealed by the 2020 census, the white population declined for the first time since 1790. The current growth in the United States is fueled by increases among ethnic minorities, especially the Hispanic population. As they settle into cities, towns, and suburban neighborhoods, the civic landscape of the future looks denser and more diverse. The opportunities are golden for neighborhood churches that respond to these trends.

Three Key Opportunities for Neighborhood Churches

As neighborhoods grew after World War II, the people in those communities started churches. Drive through any small town in the United States, and you're likely to find First Baptist, First Presbyterian, and First Methodist churches on the square, along with the courthouse. Historically, the church was the locus of community involvement. Black churches, especially, represented the hub of culture and connection in many communities. Today, this emphasis has faded within the larger culture, but the opportunities are still there to put the neighborhood church at the center of the social network. Newer neighborhoods need a more robust church-planting effort. Existing neighborhoods need a focused effort on church revitalization. The future is bright for the neighborhood church, but only if we capture the moment.

Hospitality: The Invisible Opportunity

Almost every church member believes their church is friendly. And they probably are—with people they know. However, guests are often neglected. They sit alone. No one talks to them because no one knows them. Rarely does a guest say, "This church was the friendliest group of people I've ever encountered!" At Church Answers, we've worked with hundreds of churches on improving their guest experiences. And almost every church is detached from reality when it comes to hospitality. Churches think they demonstrate hospitality. Most do not. It's an invisible opportunity because churches by and large do not see it.

There's a difference between hospitality and friendliness. You can be friendly without being hospitable. Friendliness involves being polite and kind. Hospitality means getting involved with people; it requires some sacrifice. When you sacrifice for someone, it changes your plans. When you hold the elevator, smile, or greet someone with kindness, you are demonstrating friendliness. When you stop to help someone change their flat tire, get grease on your nice shirt, and cancel the afternoon meeting, you are practicing hospitality. Offering someone a cup of coffee is friendliness. Housing a refugee is hospitality. In the words of Dustin Willis and Brandon Clements, "Ultimately the end goal of hospitality is care and healing."[12] The church should be both friendly and hospitable. But don't mistake friendliness for hospitality.

The reason churches can stand out with hospitality is because it's in short supply right now. The service industry is struggling to find enough workers. Those who are working are stretched thin, undervalued, and underpaid. Polarization in politics keeps people on edge. Motives seem more in question than in the past. Our culture, in general, has become inhospitable. Even if you think the world is coming to an end, the Bible is clear: When everything is falling apart, practice hospitality! In 1 Peter 4:7-10, the apostle Peter writes:

> The end of the world is coming soon. Therefore, be earnest and disciplined in your prayers. Most important of all, continue to show deep love for each other, for love covers a multitude of sins. Cheerfully share your home with those who need a meal or a place to stay. God has given each of you a gift from his great variety of spiritual gifts. Use them well to serve one another.

In other words, practice hospitality!

Hospitality is one of the most underappreciated and under-rated spiritual gifts. Take a moment and consider your church budget. Does your church value hospitality? If so, it should be a well-resourced ministry of the church. Don't cut the coffee budget to save money. Use it to equip people for hospitality. When was the last time you did hospitality training and equipping? Most churches have lost sight of this remarkable spiritual gift. It's largely invisible, and it needs to be brought out into the open.

Neighborhood churches can use hospitality to be a bright spot in a dark culture, and they can stand out compared to larger churches or megachurches in that regard. When someone goes into a large group setting such as a ballpark or a concert venue, he or she expects a level of anonymity. The larger the church venue, the lower the expectation of being noticed and greeted. Those expectations aren't wrong—it's just the reality of a large group gathering. But when someone walks into a neighborhood church, the smaller venue creates an expectation of being noticed and greeted. Guests expect to be shown hospitality.

Neighborhood churches must be *better* at hospitality to meet these expectations. The good news is that this goal can be accomplished through personal attention. Sit next to someone new. Walk with them around the campus. Invite them to lunch. Get their contact information and call them the following week. Neighborhood churches can assimilate guests through hospitality and delight people without disrupting their comfort level.[13] A smaller venue creates a greater expectation of hospitality but also a greater opportunity to practice hospitality. But you have to make it a priority. It won't just happen.

Real Estate: The Financial Opportunity

"What's next?" I asked the executive pastor. "You've accomplished so much as a church. Do you have something else on the horizon?"

"We need to replace the carpet in the hallways," he replied. "The cost will be around $1 million."

After I recovered from sticker shock, I realized what he was saying. The church had a large amount of deferred maintenance across their campus, and replacing the carpet was just the tip of the iceberg.

This church has a strong reputation and a long history of successful ministry. Their annual budget is north of $10 million. Yet their aging facilities were swallowing them whole.

"We're struggling to retain young families. They don't want the massive facility their parents built. I'm not sure what's next, other than replacing the carpet."

According to one source, 90 percent of the cost of owning a building occurs after construction. In other words, "your building that cost $1 million to build will cost you $9 million to own and operate over its useful life."[14] There are cases of megachurches building $100 million campuses. Maintaining such a structure will cost $1 billion over time. Some of these large churches will be able to keep up with the expenses. Others will not. The smaller campuses of most neighborhood churches create more of an opportunity than most people realize. Some might view the smaller footprint and limited parking as a hurdle. Sometimes it is. But more times than not, these neighborhood campuses represent landlocked gold.

Because many of them were built when people wanted churches in their community, they are often located strategically and centrally. A reasonably sized campus in a strategic location creates a tremendous opportunity. Neighborhood churches are situated where people live, and they can sustain the inevitable ups and downs of church finances. Mega campuses require mega crowds. Without a full room, those massive auditoriums can feel lifeless. Mega campuses require a mega budget. Deferred maintenance is a serious risk to long-term viability. The manageable real estate of a neighborhood campus is one of the greatest assets for the long-term health of a neighborhood church. Can smaller campuses fall into disrepair? Certainly. I've toured many of them. But getting out of the deferred maintenance hole is a more feasible endeavor at a campus of three acres as opposed to a campus of three hundred acres.

Scale: The Cultural Opportunity

Two aspects of scale work to the advantage of the neighborhood church. First, because there are neighborhood churches in just about every community already, a massive Great Commission and Great Commandment movement could be ignited if even a portion of them were to regain health and become active outposts for the Kingdom of God. Second, the scaled-down size of most neighborhood churches can be utilized to great benefit.

Regional churches are designed to appeal to a broader base of society. At the time they were built, such models made sense. Building big was in vogue, and the size of the church was an attraction in itself. My father tells a story about his own father taking a family vacation to Houston just to see the newly opened Astrodome. They drove all the way from South Alabama to look at the behemoth stadium and then went home. My children would think I was insane for attempting such a "vacation." But throughout the 1960s and into the 1990s, bigger was attractive for many.

Large, regional churches have their place, and many will continue to minister successfully. There is something to the economies of scale in a large church. They have the resources and facilities to do things that smaller churches could never even attempt. But it's time to release neighborhood churches from the notion that infinite expansion is even possible, much less desirable. Indeed, no church can sustain exponential growth year after year. Not every church has the potential to become a megachurch. Not every church *should* become a megachurch.

As I mentioned in the introduction, the average American drives less than fifteen minutes to church. This statistic represents data from before the pandemic and the work-from-home movement. The drive is no longer worth the distance for many people to attend church. Many churches moved to regional locations near major interstates at the height of the church growth movement. At the time, such practices were common and represented the prevailing wisdom of the experts. But the culture is shifting from *commuter* to *community*. The population growth is moving away from large, urban cores and shifting into the surrounding neighborhoods.[15] The main driver of this shift is the desire for a shorter (if any) commute.[16]

The Baby Boomers came of age when their parents used the burgeoning highway system to travel to areas of work, commerce, and recreation. Though many people still drive to such places, the culture is shifting to bring work, commerce, and recreation out to the suburbs. Thus, a neighborhood church location is one of the best Kingdom assets in North America.

Megachurches are a Baby Boomer phenomenon. They grew as the Boomers came of age. Like larger planets in our solar system, megachurches have a greater gravitational pull. They have more guests and garner more attention than neighborhood churches.

Prior to the pandemic, the largest 10 percent of churches had 60 percent of the worshipers.[17] To what degree will generational and cultural changes contribute to a move toward smaller churches? Not at all, unless those churches work to capture the opportunity. People will not flock to smaller churches just because.

But the opportunity *is* there. The good news for neighborhood churches is that a small amount of growth is enough to build a lot of momentum. Incremental gains feel like leaps forward. Each new family is the talk of the church. Can the neighborhood church reach the younger generations, specifically Millennials and their children? I believe so. Now is the time to begin.

Millennials are buying homes at a completely unexpected pace. The nation's largest generation, almost half of whom are nonwhite, is settling into home ownership and will bolster demand for the next decade.[18] In addition, Millennials and their families are moving out of larger cities and into denser suburban areas.[19] With this migration comes an incredible opportunity. The neighborhood church that welcomes them with hospitality has the potential to keep them.

Capturing the Opportunity to Grow

Many neighborhood churches stopped growing years ago. Unfortunately, they became *destination points* for the committed faithful who moved out of the neighborhood but still attended the church, rather than drawing in new people from the neighborhood. But there is hope. For many churches, the addition of a few families would change the entire culture of the congregation. The median church size is about seventy-five people. If a typical church sets the goal of growing by one family a quarter, it will add thirty-two people in three years, reaching attendance of 107 and a growth rate of 43 percent.[20] Growing by one family every three months is a reasonable goal for just about any church. Why not your church?

It's one thing to recognize an opportunity and another thing to capture it. Proverbs 4:5 says we must "get wisdom." Wisdom means applying God's standards to real life. Wise people *act* on the knowledge they gain. God honors those who *go get it*. When God gives you the knowledge to know what to do, he also gives you the responsibility to work to attain it. The bottom line is that your church will not grow without hard work. Neighborhood churches have enormous potential, perhaps as much now as when many of them were started decades ago. Potential becomes reality only through effort. And think of how rewarding this work will be. You can expand the Kingdom of God in your own neighborhood.

Perhaps you are wondering what can be done at your church specifically. I believe God can work through any congregation, regardless of budget, resources, location, or size. Every neighborhood deserves a healthy church. In the next chapter, I will examine the marks of a healthy neighborhood church. I believe God has a bright future for you and your church. It's time to get into better spiritual shape to handle future growth. Let's get to work!

3

The Marks of a Healthy Neighborhood Church

RANDY'S LAUGH ECHOED in the church every Sunday. He called everyone "brother" and "sister" and truly meant it. He had an imposing physique, but his smile was disarming. The only bristly part about him was his long, white beard. Randy could probably crush you with his hands, but instead he would embrace you with his powerful arms and lovingly squeeze the breath out of you.

One Sunday, Randy brought several people from India to church. He was always bringing people, but this Sunday was different.

"Who are the guests?" I asked one of our greeters.

"I don't know. I think Randy brought them."

"Do they speak English?"

"Not that I can tell."

The group looked confused, so I asked Randy about his friends.

"Brother Sam, I was driving around in the church bus this morning, and I saw them at the bus stop. So I asked if they wanted to go to church, and they all got on."

The engineering students from the local university thought they were headed to the park together, but instead they ended up at our church.

If someone looked different, talked different, or acted different, Randy would gravitate toward them. He had a heart for people in need. For example, he had befriended a single mom and her daughter, who herself was a single mom. The daughter was caring for the child of one of her friends, who had dropped off the baby and left town. Because of Randy's constant kindness, both women eventually accepted Christ.

"You should baptize them!" I urged Randy.

"No way. I'm not worthy, and I don't want to be in front of everyone."

"No, you'd be great."

I kept pushing him until he acquiesced.

On the morning of the baptism, Randy was a nervous, sweaty mess, but his smile was larger than his laugh was loud. His introduction of the two women was beautiful. Their testimonies were inspiring. The church cheered.

Then, as Randy stepped out of the baptistry, he stumbled forward and had a massive heart attack. Sadly, he never regained consciousness and died the next day.

Later, when I visited his widow, I apologized for pushing him to perform the baptism. Had nerves and excitement caused the heart attack? I felt an incredible amount of guilt. But I'll never forget her reply.

"God foreordained his heart attack. It was going to happen

then, no matter what. He died being obedient to God, and that's what is most important."

Then it hit me. Randy's faithfulness meant that his last words on earth were "in the name of the Father, the Son, and the Holy Spirit." And the next words he heard were, "Well done, my good and faithful servant."

Randy taught me how to live with an all-out passion for the gospel—and how to approach death ready to collapse into the arms of Jesus.

Growing a Healthy Neighborhood Church: The Marks of Success

Randy embodied many of the marks of a healthy believer: selfless, kind, joyful, and obedient. Of course, he wasn't perfect. The body of Christ, the church, is made up of individual members at varying stages of health and maturity.

Drawing conclusions about any one person's spiritual health is difficult, much less that of an entire church. For example, if a church of fifty mature believers grows by adding fifty new believers, then the church would double in size, but half the people would be new to the faith. Such a church will have signs of immaturity because of all the new believers, but it might still be a relatively healthy church. I recognize the challenge of cataloging the features of a healthy neighborhood church. What follows are general guidelines rather than a definitive list.

Woven into the Fabric of the Neighborhood

Every neighborhood looks different. Like a variety of garments, each one has its own fabric. The church should be one of the threads that holds the community together. A healthy neighborhood church will be one of the key factors that keeps the community from unraveling.

God designed local churches to have local influence. A church's influence may extend beyond the neighborhood, but this macro level influence is not its primary mission. The purpose of any one church is to minister at the micro level of the immediate surrounding community. Not everyone in the neighborhood will agree with the church's doctrine, but the majority should recognize and value the church's contribution. God's people should be the "upright citizens" mentioned in Proverbs 11:11, who are "good" for their community and "make it prosper." The people of the church should be so ingrained in the neighborhood that ministry to their neighbors is a natural part of their lifestyle. The church is called to be the bridge between a skeptical society and the spiritual life of Jesus. When this bridge is built, the church becomes an irresistible influence in the neighborhood.[1] Perhaps Tim Keller best sums up this thought with a question: "If you and your church were to disappear off the face of the earth tomorrow, would anyone in the community around you notice you were gone?"[2]

The pastor of Southpoint Fellowship (the same church mentioned in the introduction) told me about a recent incident at the church. A young man attended a worship service for the first time. Assuming he was there with a friend, the pastor did not immediately approach him. But after the service, he noticed the young man looking around as if he didn't know what to do next.

"I'm assuming you're new," the pastor said as he introduced himself.

"Yes, it's my first Sunday in church."

"Any church or this church?"

"I've never been to any church."

"What brings you here?"

"I live across the street, and I noticed how you serve the

homeless people every Saturday. I figured any church serving *every* Saturday had to be worth a look on Sunday."

Southpoint was creating a force of irresistible influence through their ministry in the community. What would happen if they disappeared overnight? Everyone in the neighborhood would miss them. They are a thread that ties the community together.

Ministries Uniquely Tailored to the Neighborhood

I recently purchased a couple of jackets that fit me great except the sleeves were slightly too long. I looked up a tailor in my neighborhood named Riccardo Mastroianni. He grew up in Italy and mastered his craft working with his father in Rome. As a young adult, he came to the United States and brought his skills to our area. He has decades of experience perfecting the techniques of tailoring. Before I walked into his shop, he knew nothing of me. But he quickly figured out exactly how to help me. Mastroianni applied the principles of his craft to my individual request.

Every neighborhood is different, with a unique set of challenges and problems. In the same way a tailor can use general techniques and apply them to a certain piece of clothing, Scripture contains principles that can be applied to specific contexts. The neighborhood church can tailor ministries to the exact needs of the surrounding community, personalizing their work in ways that large, regional churches cannot. The regional church is built on the concept that people from several neighborhoods and communities will gravitate toward a common experience. There is value in this model, but the regional church cannot possibly create unique ministries for every neighborhood represented in their congregation. That's the role of the neighborhood church. It can exist solely to meet the needs of the community, precisely tailoring ministries to match the challenges of those who live in proximity to the campus.

A healthy neighborhood church doesn't ask, "How can we be the best church in the area?" but rather, "How can we be the best church *for* the neighborhood?"[3] Quality and excellence are achieved through the tailoring of ministries. We could have the best design, highest quality fabric, or most respected brand, but if the jacket doesn't fit, it is of little value to the one who wants to wear it. The neighborhood church may not be able to compete with the wow factor of programming at a larger church, but the burden of competition is unnecessary. The neighborhood church excels not in competition at the macro level but in customizing ministries at the micro level.

Leaders Directly Connected to the Community Power Grid

Jerry is an accountant and a widely respected community leader. He is also a key member at First Methodist Church. He cringed when the local homeowner's association asked him to serve on the board. The only meetings more rancorous than church business meetings are HOA meetings. The outgoing president had assaulted another member in an argument about the pool cameras. Though the bar for leadership was set low, tensions were sky-high. Jerry knew serving on the board was going to require more than just his time. Reputations were on the line.

Everyone knew Jerry was a faithful follower of Christ. He had accepted Christ about forty years ago, through a Fellowship of Christian Athletes event, and had been outspoken about his faith ever since. He viewed the HOA opportunity through the lens of the gospel. Many who served on the board were power brokers in the community, and few of them attended church or had a relationship with Christ. Jerry prayed diligently about opportunities to show and share the love of Christ through his time on the board.

A healthy neighborhood church has members like Jerry. Often, their ministry is through their influence in the community. This ministry may not be a formal program or an event at the church. It's more of a culture of service within the church that spills into the neighborhood. Does the community's power structure value the participation of church members? How strong is the church's connection to this larger community power grid? These connections can come through the pastors or elders of the church, or through lifelong local church members, as is often the case in an established church. When a neighborhood church is disconnected from the community power grid, it becomes harder to shine the light of Christ into the lives of the area's influencers. Plugging into the grid amplifies the message and influence of the neighborhood church.

The Church's Story Becomes Part of the Community's History

When a neighborhood church weaves itself into the fabric of the neighborhood, over time it will become intertwined with the history of the community. In my late twenties and early thirties, I pastored a church with a historical marker in the front yard. Murray, Kentucky, has a deep and involved community history, and First Baptist Church is part of it. The history of the community cannot be told without the church's contribution to the story. Sure, there is plenty to critique about how the church interacted with the community over its 150 year history. There were several colorful characters along the way. For example, Pastor Boyce Taylor was put in jail for holding services during the 1919 flu pandemic.[4] There is an entire room in the church building dedicated to preserving the history of the church.

What I learned to love about First Baptist was how the church valued the community history more than the history of the church itself. The people are proud to be part of the story in Murray and not just their own thing. Though the heritage room has a museum-level number of artifacts, the care taken to preserve history is more about the church's place in the community. A healthy neighborhood church will want to tell their story in the context of the community's story.

Intertwined with Other Local Churches

If each church is a thread in the fabric of the community, then all the church threads should connect to make the community stronger. Healthy neighborhood churches are not isolated from one another. Though there will always be doctrinal distinctions, these differences should not separate churches into a series of spiritual islands in the neighborhood. Building bridges, rather than burning them, is a key indicator of a healthy church.

Another neighborhood church is about a mile from my church in West Bradenton. Westside Christian is often confused with our church, and the confusion is a point of mutual amusement for Tim Boyd, their pastor, and me. He and I have become good friends. We both have side gigs. I run a company, and he is a stand-up comedian.[5]

On a recent Sunday, I learned we were out of Communion supplies. Of course, we could have postponed the Lord's Supper to another week, but I did not feel right doing so. Westside Christian has Communion every week, so I called Tim.

"Wait, let me get this straight. The Baptist church is calling on the Christian church to help with Communion. I'm never gonna let you live this one down."

There is a long history of conflict between the two denominations that dates to the pioneer era of the United States. For Tim and me, our differences are more of a way to joke with each other than hurt each other. We were grateful for the emergency supply of Communion cups. And West Bradenton Baptist was happy to advertise Tim's comedy event. The connection between our churches is no laughing matter, except when it is.

A Place to Serve, Not Pull In Congregants

A healthy neighborhood church views the community as a place to serve, not as a resource to pull in potential congregants. When the church growth movement picked up steam in the 1970s, the popular idea arose that God values numerical growth in local churches, and declining churches fall short of God's expectations.[6] Numerical growth remains the primary metric of success among evangelicals.[7] Healthy neighborhood churches should grow numerically, and declining churches should take numerical drops seriously. But the neighborhood should not be viewed simply as a resource to grow the church. Rather, the church is God's resource to grow the neighborhood spiritually.

Healthy churches will grow spiritually and numerically, but the numerical growth results from the church's work in the community. Faithful presence in the neighborhood occurs through a cycle of listening, discerning, and acting.[8] First, we must listen to understand the key issues and problems. Discernment is necessary to understand how the church should respond, and the church acts on this discernment by serving the neighborhood in a way that glorifies God. When we view the neighborhood merely as a resource for church growth, we are not seeking to love the people around us and see them flourish. Remember, the neighborhood does not exist to help the church grow. The church exists to help the neighborhood grow. Numerical growth is not a means to an end; it's a natural outcome of successful ministry in the neighborhood.

The Church Building as a Shared Community Resource

Many established neighborhood churches have at least one person who can tell the story of every tile, screw, wire, brick, and shingle. These people know every intricacy of the building because their sweat and blood put them in place. Can someone fix the circuit board on the elevator? Yup, we have a guy. Who can lay the new laminate in the kids' hall? A team will be there on Tuesday. Need a new toilet? Somebody has one in the truck. This connection to the building is both physical and spiritual.

Longtime members in an established neighborhood church identify with the buildings as much as they do with each other. The buildings are part of the discipleship process, because people connect their spiritual growth to a certain place and time. This spiritual connection is a positive thing. The building is part of what draws people to the church, where they can then be discipled and grow in Christ.

However, the connection can become unhealthy if members of a neighborhood church start to believe that they—rather than God—own the building. Unhealthy neighborhood churches tend to assert a right of ownership in the building that can draw them away from the mission of God.[9] A healthy neighborhood church will view the building and campus as a shared community resource.

Chains on parking lots and members-only signs are good indicators that a neighborhood church has lost its sense of mission. Do local schools utilize your church building? Do neighbors congregate on your lawn? Do children use the playground? I understand the issues of security and liability. We have measures in place for both at my church. But I believe church policies and practices should tend toward an open campus model rather than a closed campus model. One of the easiest ways to start revitalizing

THE MARKS OF A HEALTHY NEIGHBORHOOD CHURCH

a neighborhood church is to let the community know that your campus and building are open to the neighbors.

The Neighborhood of One

God's Kingdom grows one neighbor at a time. Jesus spoke to the masses, but he always had time for individuals. In Mark 10:42-45, Jesus defines the standard of greatness in the Kingdom: The first shall be last, and the last shall be first. On the road to Jericho with his disciples, Jesus puts this principal into action for his followers to see (Mark 10:46-52).

The road to Jericho was well-traveled and ideal for begging. Bartimaeus, a beggar who was also blind, cries out when he hears that Jesus is passing by. The people try to shut him up. But he will not be deterred. He throws off his coat and runs to Jesus.

Don't miss the significance of this tiny detail. His coat was all that he owned, his entire net worth. Unlike the rich, young ruler in Mark 10:17-22, who would not give up *anything* for Jesus, Bartimaeus gave up *everything* for him. Would you cast aside your entire net worth to meet Jesus?

Bartimaeus runs through the crowd with total abandon, no doubt bumping into people and creating a chaotic scene. Mark 10:49 is one of the most powerful verses in the entire Bible: "When Jesus heard him, he stopped." Human destiny hangs in the balance. Jesus was on his way to Jerusalem to save humanity. Would he sacrifice the one for the many? No. He stops.

We live in a maddening world of go, go, go. Travel sports, smartphones, social media—the world never stops. We're all on that busy road to Jericho. On the shoulder, people are hurting, waiting for someone to notice, to stop, to help. Will we stop like Jesus did? If anyone had a reason *not* to stop, it was Jesus at that moment. But he had time to meet the needs of the one.

Jesus asks Bartimaeus, "What do you want me to do for you?"

It's an odd question. The answer is obvious. The man is blind and wants to see. But Jesus often asked obvious questions to elicit a faith response. He wanted to know whether Bartimaeus truly believed.

"My Rabbi," Bartimaeus responds, "I want to see!"

Jesus healed the blind man physically, but Bartimaeus received spiritual sight as well. How do we know?

Jesus acknowledges that faith was what healed Bartimaeus's blindness, but something more is evident in the text. Now that he could see, Bartimaeus was free to go wherever he wanted. Jesus simply told him to go. So where does Bartimaeus go? "He followed Jesus down the road" (Mark 10:52). His way was now the way of Jesus. Perhaps Bartimaeus followed Jesus all the way to the cross, seeing with his healed eyes what he already knew to be true in his healed soul.

The best way to grow the Kingdom is one person at a time—like Jesus often did. The most important mark of a healthy neighborhood church is the willingness to stop and make room for the one. If every member of every neighborhood church were willing to stop for just one other person, I believe it would ignite an incredible movement of God. I believe it can happen. A neighborhood of one will become a neighborhood of many.

4

A New Framework to Understand Neighborhood Churches

THE OPENING SENTENCE in our consultation report was blunt, but we had to tell the church the truth: "The status quo will lead your church toward death in about five years."

The congregation didn't feel the urgency of the crisis. They had about two hundred people in regular attendance, but they were losing an average of one person per week. Because it was an older congregation, some were passing away. Others could no longer attend due to health issues. A few were leaving out of frustration because the church was going nowhere.

As we walked the campus with the pastor, the two-story stone sanctuary cast a long shadow in the late afternoon summer sun. Those stones had stood the test of time, weathering many storms. The building was solid; it was not going anywhere. The people were just as immovable as the stones, but they were fading quickly.

Despite the obvious challenges, Pastor Derick was hopeful.

"We've been in this neighborhood more than one hundred years. This building is a fixture here. We assume people will show up because of the beauty of the campus, but they don't. It's time we started going to them."

After six months of outreach efforts, the church managed to stop the decline. The number of weekly guests doubled. More importantly, the congregation now viewed the church as a vehicle to send people *into* the neighborhood, rather than simply a beautiful destination for people in the neighborhood.

A Typology of Church Revitalization

In my book *The Church Revitalization Checklist*, I introduce several categories of churches in need of revitalization. These categories were derived from a Church Answers research project in which we asked church revitalizers to categorize their work. We received hundreds of responses from both pastors and lay leaders. The figures below represent the percentages of churches in each category as reported by those respondents:

- *Geriatric churches* (40 percent): The median age of the church's members is significantly higher than the community at large. Few families or children are present.
- *Great Omission churches* (25 percent): The church's ministries, resources, and efforts are focused inward with hardly any evangelistic efforts.
- *Ex-neighborhood churches* (15 percent): The church's membership does not reflect the community's demographics. The church is a cultural island in the neighborhood. Typically, few people from the immediate

community attend the church. Most members drive in
from other communities.

- *War-torn churches* (12 percent): These churches have a
  reputation for fighting, conflict, harsh treatment of pastors,
  and—often—schisms and splits. There is a palpable
  tension at meetings and in casual conversations around
  the church. The leaders pour most of their energy into
  mediating disputes and responding to arguments.
- *Mismatched leadership churches* (8 percent): The pastor is
  not the right leader for moving the church forward. In
  many cases, the pastor has no love for the community and
  may demean the people who live there.[1]

These general categories can apply to any established church,
not just neighborhood churches. Additionally, the percentages represent the dominant problem in the church. A church can struggle
with more than one of these issues. But if we focus specifically
on neighborhood churches, an additional typology emerges. The
problems within neighborhood churches are often deeper than
what is described in the "ex-neighborhood churches" category.
What kinds of neighborhood churches exist, and why do many
of them struggle?

A New Framework: The Different Types of Neighborhood Churches

Neighborhood churches are typically small or medium-size congregations, though it is possible—but rare—to have a neighborhood megachurch. African American churches in particular can
be both large and woven into the neighborhood. Discriminatory
practices such as redlining—where banks did not make loans to
Black homebuyers in certain neighborhoods—contributed to the

isolation of ethnic neighborhoods. The church often became a place where people found affirmation, identity, and a celebration of their inherent value.

"You'd show up to Black church, and while you were called racial epithets throughout the week, at church you were Deacon Jones," one interviewee summarized in a *Christianity Today* article.[2] This dynamic created an environment in which Black churches grew to large sizes within specific neighborhoods.

There are other cases of large neighborhood churches, but most are fairly small. Neighborhood churches can be of any ethnic mix, whether multiethnic or monoethnic. They can also be of any denominational or doctrinal background. There are poor neighborhood churches and affluent neighborhood churches. Young with families and older without children—just about any generational breakdown is found in these churches. The variety of neighborhood churches makes them difficult to categorize. The framework presented here is less about membership demographics and more about the perspectives of both the church and the community.

		Perspective of the Church	
		Open	Closed
Perspective of the Community	Included	Engaged	Isolated
	Excluded	Removed	Detached

The obvious goal for neighborhood churches is to be in the top left quadrant—open and engaged with the neighborhood. Unfortunately, far too many neighborhood churches fall into the other categories. Most smaller churches are not focused on growth, and they struggle to have a robust presence in the community.[3] They tend to be more inwardly focused, which translates to being isolated, removed, and detached from their neighborhoods. The ray of hope is that any incremental improvement in community engagement will likely yield good results. Let's take a deeper dive into this framework by first explaining the community and church perspectives.

Perspective of the Church

A neighborhood church can be either open or closed to the community. An *open* neighborhood church expects visitors, welcomes guests, and actively invites people to their worship services and groups. An open church allows the community to utilize their facility during the week. Community members are often on the church property, even if they are not official members of the church. When a neighborhood church is open, the congregation wants members of the community to be present at the church however and whenever possible.

A *closed* neighborhood church finds ways to keep the community at a distance. Chains block off access to the parking lot. Giant signs warn trespassers and threaten vehicle towing. Members don't invite neighbors, friends, and family to worship services. The building is reserved for members only, and people from the neighborhood are rarely found on campus for any reason. The closed church makes it known—whether intentionally or unintentionally—that their neighbors are not welcome. Sometimes these churches have literal signs reading "Keep Off the Grass." As you might imagine, the sense of mission in such churches is weak or nonexistent.

Perspective of the Community

The community will want to be included or excluded from the life of the church. When the community wants to be included, local schools will call about using the church's facilities for graduation. Neighborhood families will bring their children to play on the church playground. Churches with a desirable day care or a school will have waiting lists. The neighbors will view the open church as a place of healing and prayer, even if they don't attend services there. The pastors and leaders of open neighborhood churches are often asked to give an invocation at community events.

When a community wants to exclude the neighborhood church, it's usually because of a scandal or squabble. One church in a Southern state, for example, went so far as to sue the local government over a particular issue. In other cases, the local government is opposed to religion and acts aggressively toward churches in the community. This kind of antagonism—whether started by the church or by local officials—often prompts members of the community to avoid the church. As the above grid indicates, the perspectives of the community and the church converge to create four categories of neighborhood churches. Let's explore them in greater depth now.

Engaged with the Neighbors

I introduced Pastor Derick earlier in this chapter. Within six months of our consultation with his church, they had stemmed their decline and were beginning to heal. Guests from the neighborhood were coming each week, and the tone of the church had changed significantly. What happened? Can a turnaround start in as little as six months? It can. I asked Pastor Derick what made the difference.

"A box of cereal," he replied.

"You will have to explain this one."

"We decided to take a chance and be clever. Our hope was to make a memorable impression."

"What does cereal have to do with being memorable?" I asked.

He explained how they started going door-to-door with mini

boxes of Lucky Charms in gift bags containing information about the church. They told people who answered the door, "We're lucky to be your neighbor," and handed them the gift bag. The outreach effort was a hit with both the church and the neighbors.

"Everyone got a good laugh," the pastor said.

Going door-to-door can feel intrusive, but this effort was disarming, both for the church and the neighbors. The church moved outward, and the neighborhood responded positively. This was in large part because the idea was so clever, but also because the church was willing to bring fun into the mix.

"For six months, we went door-to-door," Pastor Derick continued. "Sometimes we brought prayer cards. We brought a small box of chocolate for Valentine's Day. The effort didn't cost much, and frankly, it's some of the best use of funds in the recent history of our church."

Engagement happens when the church is open to the community and the community wants to be included in the life of the church. In most cases, this doesn't happen naturally. It takes a concerted outreach effort from the church.

The engaged church has an ongoing relationship with the community. It is more than a one-time outreach effort or special event. The church will find ways to be active in the rhythms of the community. It will sponsor sports teams and participate in leagues. Partnerships will form between the church and other local nonprofit organizations. You'll notice the church logo at local schools or fundraisers because of sponsorships.

When the church engages with its neighbors, it becomes woven into the fabric of the community. People feel the presence of the church in the community. They know the church's location, even if they've never been inside the building. The engaged church will do regular outreach in the community. These efforts can be clever, like the one that Pastor Derick tried, but they must always be genuine. Most people can tell when you are reaching out to them with a genuine heart, even if they don't quite understand why you're doing it.

The engaged community also seeks help from the church. Healthy engagement is a two-way street. Not only is the church reaching outward, but the community is reaching to the church. The elementary school calls to use the church facility for their graduation ceremony. When a natural disaster hits, the community asks the church to be a shelter. But this engagement extends beyond the building and campus. The community often calls upon members of the church. Engaged church members serve on local boards and participate in community activities, and the neighborhood recognizes them as representatives of the church. The engaged community considers the pastor as part of the leadership structure of the neighborhood. Leaders in the church are viewed as having a positive impact on the neighborhood, and the community actively seeks their participation in key decisions and local efforts. The engaged community sees the church as part of the neighborhood narrative. The story of the neighborhood will include the story of the church. When people discuss their community, the engaged church is a talking point.

Isolated from the Neighbors

An isolated church is an unusual case. This group is likely the smallest category of neighborhood churches, but they do exist. The isolation is not accidental on behalf of the church. These congregations take active steps to avoid their neighbors. The community may want to include the church, but the church is closed to the community. How does this situation arise? These churches can take many forms, but the situation most commonly occurs with a historic church.

First Baptist Church in a particular small town has a rich history, going back almost two hundred years. The campus is situated in the heart of a neighborhood just east of the downtown square. Over the last ten years, community leaders have attempted to bring the pastor into local discussions about a variety of issues, but he puts them off saying he doesn't have time.

Indeed, this pastor has other fish to fry. He is currently caught in the middle of quite a fight. The church is divided doctrinally, and all his energy goes to mediating between two large factions in the church. A split seems inevitable, but he is doing everything he can to hold the church together. Though the community is aware of some tension in the church, most people are not in tune with the nuances of the congregation's theological squabbles. As such, the community leaders are baffled by the isolation of a church that was once the most active congregation in the neighborhood.

This isolation has prompted the community to believe that the pastor is likely the main culprit, but the truth is the opposite. He is trying to bridge the gaps within his church, but in so doing, he cut off the church's bridge to the community. Because the pastor is not originally from this town, some lifelong and generational community leaders are becoming skeptical. They keep reaching out and getting rebuffed. Given the church's internal battles, the pastor believes his time must be spent there, but the people who could help him solve the problem are outside the church. These leaders are also churchgoers in other congregations. They are trusted in the community, and their presence might calm the agitators. But the pastor has allowed the church to become closed to the community for a season, believing the internal battles would give the church a bad reputation if they were known in the community.

As you can imagine, that pastor didn't last much longer in the church. When another congregation offered him a position, the greener grass was too much to turn down. He left the church isolated from the neighborhood and in a terrible state of tension. Ultimately, the congregation split, and one group joined the Methodist church on the downtown square. Even though the pastor's motives were pure, most in the church and in the town blamed him for the split. As an outsider who no longer lived in the community, he was an easy scapegoat. His big strategic mistake was turning down offers for help during his ten years at the church. Would the church have avoided a split if they had been more open to the community? It's tough to know. But isolation rarely works out for the church or the neighborhood.

Removed by the Neighbors

The concept of guarding your reputation is found throughout Scripture, and for good reason. What takes years to build can be lost in a moment. The wisdom of Proverbs includes this insight: "Choose a good reputation over great riches; being held in high esteem is better than silver or gold" (Proverbs 22:1). A leadership scandal can set back a church's reputation for a long time. One neighborhood church in the mid-South serves as a warning.

For decades, this church was the go-to house of worship in the community. They grew larger than the average neighborhood church and had a regional reputation for solid growth year after year. But the church experienced a terrible scandal involving child safety. What happened was awful enough, but then the church tried to cover it up. The local news caught wind of how church leaders were dismissing the concerns of parents and not being forthright on the facts of the case. The issue blew up, and the church was in the news for several weeks. Within a few days, the church's reputation was ruined, and families left in a mass exodus. The older group remaining in the church still had the resources and the desire to be open to the neighborhood, but the community excluded the church in dramatic fashion. The pastor left because of the scandal, and the church struggled for several years to find someone qualified to lead the congregation.

In this instance, the church deserved to be excluded. Such is not always the case. Some places in North America are not as welcoming to religious organizations, specifically the church. In these cases, a winsome spirit and a willingness to persevere are necessary. A missionary mindset is required to break through in neighborhoods more inclined to exclude the church. For example, our team at Church Answers worked with a church in the upper Midwest, where the local government was attempting to use eminent domain to take a portion of their parking lot and use it as parking for the neighborhood park. It was an egregious case, and the church was in the difficult spot of fighting some of the people they wanted to reach. The pastor and the church handled the situation with incredible grace but also had to act firmly and shrewdly to sustain the church's ministry.

Though the specifics of these cases are not the norm, many neighborhood churches are excluded from their community even as they are open to reaching their community. This conundrum is not insurmountable, but it takes extra effort to build several bridges between the church, the people living around the church, and key community leaders. Neighborhood churches that commit to this effort will likely experience an incredible payoff over the course of a few years. The time frame may be longer than most would desire, but the effort is worth it.

Detached from the Neighbors

Detachment occurs through the pathways of antagonism and apathy. I mentioned earlier a church that sued their local government.

The case involved issues not related to religious liberty or persecution. The pastor was a known instigator and seemed to enjoy the notoriety that accompanied the reputation. He didn't always distinguish between positive and negative attention. The church was small, and it did grow as a result of the lawsuit when some sympathizers to the pastor's cause joined the congregation. But the church became detached from the community and antagonistic toward its neighbors. Tensions rose and people soon began avoiding interaction with anyone from the church. Sadly, the members were almost proud of their detachment. They saw it as a mark of their purity. Of course, this tension and detachment isn't healthy, nor does it benefit the Kingdom of God.

While antagonism draws attention, apathy tends to go unnoticed. Detachment through apathy is an off-the-radar occurrence. When a church has little desire to be open to the community, seemingly content to be a stale and neutral presence there, neighbors will hardly notice the church's existence, and the church's campus simply blends into the landscape. Though I don't have hard data to back it up, I believe this kind of neighborhood church is the most prevalent. There are far more small churches across North America than large churches. Drive through any neighborhood in most cities, suburbs, and small towns, and you will find a variety of small churches. They anchor a piece of real estate but are otherwise invisible to the community. These churches hardly know their neighbors, and the neighbors don't know—or care—much about the churches. Should even a small number of these detached churches wake up and reach out, a large-scale movement would occur. What if every neighborhood had just one church that decided to become an active part of the community? The dots of those churches would connect in ways that would build an incredible network within God's Kingdom. Why not? I believe it can happen.

Open, Included, and Multiplying

What if a box of Lucky Charms changed everything for your neighborhood church? Perhaps the question seems naive. There are numerous issues and problems that militate against a movement of neighborhood churches. Indeed, in the next two chapters, I will discuss some common myths of neighborhood churches and explore the challenges they face. The erosion of religious liberty is real. The numerical decline of congregations is real. The omission of evangelism is real. The external threats and the internal problems present major hurdles to the future health of neighborhood churches—indeed, all churches. But I believe a simple change of perspective can make a significant, positive difference. If a neighborhood church will actively pursue an open engagement with the community, I believe many neighborhoods will want to include that church. Not every church will make it, I know. Not every church will reach outward. But your church can. You can lead this effort and be part of a multiplication effect. Grab a box of cereal and let's go.

5

Myths of the Neighborhood Church

THE SNOWSTORM caught me by surprise. Several inches had blanketed the hotel parking lot while I slept. Michigan in February is cold. I lived in the Midwest for a portion of my life, but after my years in Florida, winter was not at the forefront of my mind. But of course the snow did not stop the locals from their daily routines. I made my way to the church on roads filled with cautious rush-hour drivers.

The leaders of the church impressed me with their hospitality. They provided a constant replenishment of coffee and snacks. They were the consulting client, but they made me feel like an honored guest on their campus. In their minds, I was. Their kindness was genuine. With some church consultations, it is difficult to narrow down a large number of needed recommendations. In other cases, the church has taught me more about what they're doing right than I could find that they were doing wrong. This church fell into the latter category.

The church had recently considered relocating to a different part of town where more land was available, but ultimately they decided to stay in the neighborhood.

"Most of our people live near the church. We're landlocked, but moving would mean becoming a completely different church. We want to stay close to what we consider our mission field."

The congregation wanted to know how to continue growing as a neighborhood church—on a landlocked campus with limited parking. The location was embedded in the neighborhood, nowhere near a major road. It had been built more than sixty years ago when the neighborhood formed as an enclave of the midsize city to which it is connected. Over the years, the area had transitioned from predominantly white and middle-class to more ethnically diverse and affluent.

"We understand our limitations, but we believe these limiting factors are how and why God will work. If we relocate because we think it will make things easier for us, then we're attempting to do things through our own strength and for our own benefit. We're called to this neighborhood because it's where God put us."

I heartily agreed.

A few months later, the church decided to start a Thursday night service for people who worked on Sundays, plant a new church where they had considered relocating, and reallocate some of their capital to fund independent works with missionaries who had grown up in the church.

I loved the pastor's response when I followed up: "We didn't need more land and parking. What we needed was more local and cross-cultural ministry."

Myths can become self-fulling prophecies if you believe them long enough. They don't even have to be true to affect you and your church. This neighborhood church fit many of the stereotypes that people use to explain why growth is not occurring. They were a church with limited parking, on a landlocked campus in a difficult-to-find neighborhood location. They were also a medium-size, multigenerational church in a transitioning community that was becoming more ethnically diverse. All these factors could have been hurdles if they had believed the myths. But this church figured out they were more a picture of the future than of the past, and they moved forward with a vision for what they *could* do, rather than allowing what they couldn't do to limit them.

What are some myths about neighborhood churches? And how can neighborhood congregations move beyond those myths?

Myth: Our Church Should Grow Exponentially Every Year

Every church has limiting factors. This myth is not specific to neighborhood churches, but I start here because it is so pervasive. No church grows exponentially every year. Infinite expansion isn't possible. Even the largest churches stay at the top of the list for only about twenty years.[1] Each generation has its own group of the biggest or fastest-growing congregations. Compare any lists of the largest churches from the 1970s, 1980s, 1990s, or 2000s and you'll find different churches leading the way. By virtue of their size, big churches are constantly shifting. Some of the largest churches from past decades no longer exist. They grew rapidly, peaked, declined, and eventually disappeared.

No church should die, whether the congregation is large or small. God wants every church to be biblically faithful and grow both numerically and spiritually. The myth of exponential growth has its roots in the attention garnered by churches that grow rapidly over several years. Other pastors examine these growth models and try to emulate them. Truth be told, these churches often flourish because of demographic factors that don't necessarily transfer to different locales. Maybe they're in a fast-growth corridor of a large metropolitan area. What people tend not to examine quite as much is how many of these churches fade from the growth lists just as quickly as they arrived.

The coronavirus pandemic made many church leaders and researchers rethink how good growth occurs. The distinction may seem nuanced, but there is a difference between the mentality of multiplying disciples and that of growing a large church.[2]

People will always be attracted to institutions, organizations, and movements that are growing rapidly. I can't fault those people for gravitating toward something that is vibrant and growing. However, every case of exponential growth—whether in business, religion, or the academy—eventually reaches an *inflection point*—a "key event that dramatically changes the [organization's] trajectory."[3] The inflection point is that moment when the organization must fundamentally change how it operates if it wants to survive.

Consider Sears, Roebuck and Co., once the largest retailer in the United States. Their exponential growth began to slow in the 1980s, reached an inflection point with the emergence of Walmart on the national stage, and then hit a rapid decline until the company faced Chapter 11 bankruptcy in 2018.

It's exciting when a church grows from twenty members to forty in one year, from forty to eighty the following year, and from eighty to 160 the year after that. But ongoing exponential growth is an unachievable goal for a local church. We should celebrate this growth but not expect it to continue to accelerate year after year. Churches tend to get into trouble when they construct campuses, build infrastructure, and hire personnel with the expectation of ongoing exponential growth.

MYTHS OF THE NEIGHBORHOOD CHURCH

Myth: Limited Parking Severely Limits Our Growth

There is a point at which parking becomes a significant problem. For example, a church with a thousand-seat worship space and a parking lot that holds fifty cars will struggle because of the mismatch between its interior space and exterior footprint. Some urban churches have little to no parking, but mass transit enables people to get to the church with relative ease. Most neighborhood churches will have smaller lots, but limited parking is not an in-surmountable problem.

Churches will average 2.0 to 2.5 people per vehicle. If your parking lot is correctly sized, you will have twice as many seats in the building as spaces for vehicles in the lot. In other words, a worship space for 300 requires about 150 parking spaces. If you can't create enough parking, multiple services can solve the problem. Your worship space with multiple services may never be full, but that's only a problem if attendance drops below 40 percent of capacity—the point at which, experience shows, people start to notice the empty spots more than the occupied spaces.

For purposes of discussion, let's assume a neighborhood church wants to grow to six hundred people on a Sunday morning, but they have only 150 parking spaces and a worship space with four hundred seats. This church can achieve its goal by expanding to three worship services.

8:00 a.m. Sunday worship: 150 people on campus occupying 75 parking spaces

9:30 a.m. Sunday worship: 200 people on campus occupying 100 parking spaces

11:00 a.m. Sunday worship: 250 people on campus occupying 125 parking spaces

THE SURPRISING RETURN OF THE NEIGHBORHOOD CHURCH

Will some services feel a little light throughout the year in a worship space of four hundred seats? Yes, but that's not a huge deterrent for guests. Will the parking lot get crowded some Sundays when turnover between services doesn't happen quickly? Yes, but the energy of a full parking lot will outweigh the negative impact of not finding a spot immediately. Does this church need clear signage and a lot of parking for guests, handicapped, and seniors? Yes! But these issues are quickly resolved with some budget funds and sweat equity. If the church is willing to give up on the idea that everyone must be together in the same service, or that the worship space must be completely full, then the parking lot issues—though challenging—can be overcome. If this church were to add a Sunday evening service and another service during the week, even with only 150 parking spaces they could grow to one thousand in attendance. As I mentioned previously, no church can grow exponentially every year, but neighborhood churches can grow much larger than many envision with some sacrifice and a little creativity.

Myth: We Can't Compete with the Larger Church Down the Road

First of all, it's not a competition. I think most Christians would agree that the Kingdom of God doesn't follow zero-sum, competitive, business-oriented principles. For churches large and small, the ultimate goal is the same: bring lost people to Christ and help them find a church home where they can grow in their faith.

My church doesn't lose if your church gains. There is, after all, only one church—the body of Christ. But I understand the sentiment—if not the fear—from smaller congregations when there's a much larger congregation right down the street.

For the last several decades, the median church size has dropped while the number of people attending larger churches has increased. This trend means that smaller churches are gradually getting smaller while the biggest churches get bigger. Yet, as we will see in chapter 6, the megachurch movement has begun to wane. Most people in smaller churches may not be aware of this inflection point for megachurches and other large churches, so the fear remains, but we mustn't allow it to become a self-fulfilling prophecy.

Large, regional churches—by design—must be broad in scope. Because their reach is regional, maintaining a micro-focus on ministry is difficult. Thus they tend to be structured around programs and events. Great relationships can be formed in large churches, of course, but the predominant ministry model is driven by a "pull people in and fill the room" mentality. In a large church, a series of poorly attended worship experiences can spark panic.

Smaller churches, on the other hand, tend to be driven more by relationships. The programs and events in smaller churches are determined and assessed by their effect on relationships, rather than by how many people attend.[4] A series of poorly attended worship services may prompt some discussion but typically will not cause panic. In most small churches, you know who's missing, and you can pick up the phone and call them.

The competition between small and large churches is more perception than reality. Can small churches lose members to larger churches? Yes, it happens. But small churches can also glean members from larger churches. Some people desire the relational connections that epitomize smaller congregations. And as the majority of churchgoers want to drive less than fifteen minutes to church, many simply don't want to travel further to get to a regional church, unlike previous generations. I believe small churches have a bright future of reaching their neighbors. In chapter 8, we'll examine how such a movement can begin.

Myth: Small Size Means Small Influence

Influence can be measured by *reach* and *impact*. Reach involves how far. Impact involves how deep. When a large church pursues significant reach, their success is often determined by how many people participate.

Sometimes these churches get criticized for "focusing on the numbers." And occasionally that criticism may be well-earned. Some churches plaster their attendance figures everywhere. They show pictures of massive crowds on social media. They advertise the bigness of their ministries.

In other ways, the criticism is unwarranted. We should celebrate when thousands come to Christ, something that's not likely to happen in a single small church.

Neighborhood churches can measure their influence more by deep impact than broad reach. Whereas large, regional churches are necessarily broad in scope, smaller neighborhood churches can be laser-focused on customized ministry. For example, a large regional church might create an outreach to every police and fire station in the area. They organize a day of ministry and send out a mass of people with a broad reach. The neighborhood church is more apt to walk across the street to the police or fire station and build an ongoing relationship with the officers or firefighters. Both forms of ministry are valid. Both can have a great influence on the community.

Successful neighborhood churches may embrace a philosophy of being *strategically* small rather than *intentionally* small.[5] Strategic smallness seeks to leverage the strengths of a smaller size for greater ministry effectiveness, whereas churches that intentionally stay small betray a dangerous inward mentality.

Small size doesn't have to mean small influence. The influence of a neighborhood church will just look different from that of a larger, regional church.

Myth: We're a Vestige of the Past

One of the most dangerous mindsets in a neighborhood church is to assume that its best days are in the past. Small, established churches tend to be rooted in history and nervous about the future.[6] But hope always looks forward. In the book of Haggai, the people wanted to return to the past so badly that they lost sight of what God had in store for them. Tasked with rebuilding the Temple in Jerusalem that had been destroyed, they were disappointed that the new Temple would not have the grandeur of Solomon's Temple. Instead of *building on* the past, they were *comparing to* the past. In Haggai 2:6-7, God promises that treasures will come, and he will shake the earth and heavens to demonstrate his power. But the past was so ingrained in the people that they didn't see God's future. Memories are good. Nostalgia can make people smile. But worshiping the past is idolatry.

Symptoms of loving the past more than the future include complaining, apathy, and lack of passion. But you also cannot love the future church more than the church of today. If you do, you'll be tempted to get ahead of God. Symptoms of looking too far ahead include impatience, restlessness, and lack of contentment.

The people in Haggai were surrounded by rubble. Jerusalem had been ransacked. After starting to rebuild on the foundation of the original Temple, they stopped and did nothing for sixteen years. They became discouraged and focused on themselves. This could be the story of many neighborhood churches. In Haggai, God helps the people recognize that the Temple they are building will be better than the one in the past. God was building something beyond a physical structure. The more significant work would culminate in the coming of Jesus, who would enter the Temple they were building and become the fulfillment of it. Though they couldn't see it, they were moving forward. You don't need to retreat into the past. God is leading your church into the future.

Myth: Our Location Makes Us Invisible

There are clear advantages to location. Signage, road frontage, and ve-hicle volume can make a difference. But a church's location is not what makes it invisible. The reason that churches fall off the neighborhood's radar has more to do with a lack of mission and a lack of confidence. Small congregations can struggle with a poor self-image, feeling weak, unattractive, and limited.[7] The invisibility factor is less about location and more about self-perception. When you perceive insurmountable inadequacies in your church, you are less likely to invite neighbors, friends, and coworkers to a worship service or ministry event.

In a recent conversation with a pastor in California, he described to me how his church had overcome the perceived downsides of their location. The church was buried in a neighborhood, two odd turns off the main road. Zoning restrictions meant limited signage. But his church was not invisible. In fact, most people in the community knew precisely where the church was located. How?

"People don't drop into church anymore," he said. "Inviting people is far more successful than a strategic road location with a lot of visibility. There is another church on the main road where you must turn to get to our church. They aren't growing, and we are—mainly because we invite people to church, and they don't."

Myth: The Most Capable Pastors Lead the Largest Churches

In the 1990s, an emerging discussion addressed the desire to turn around struggling churches.[8] Church growth experts started using the term "turnaround churches," which became the precursor to the church revitalization movement of the mid-2000s. The idea was that small churches could grow again. Gen X pastors and Millennials began to sense a calling to these smaller churches, along with a vision for leading a turnaround strategy.

Today there is a solid group of pastors and church leaders willing to take on the challenges of church revitalization. Many are co-vocational or bi-vocational. Co-vocational pastors have made a strategic decision to remain in the secular workforce, regardless of whether their church can afford to pay a full-time salary. Bi-vocational pastors serve churches that cannot afford to pay a full-time salary. Everyone in these positions understands that there is no such thing as a part-time pastor. Both positions are part-time pay with full-time work.

In recent years, Baby Boomer pastors have started retiring from ministry, and there are not enough Gen X and Millennial pastors to take their places. Hiring in the church is difficult and will remain so for quite some time. But there is a strong contingent of pastors with a calling to serve neighborhood churches. Many grew up in the area, sometimes in the churches they now serve. The lure of larger churches with bigger pay packages remains, but such is the case in any profession, not just ministry. There are also those who want to exit a megachurch and focus on different approaches to leading congregations. The Millennial and Gen Z generations are the most diverse in the history of North America. Their callings within the church are just as diverse. Neighborhood churches are just as likely to land capable leaders as their larger counterparts, but only if they demonstrate a willingness to move forward.

Believing the Myths Makes You the Stereotype

In April 2022, Gulfport Presbyterian Church, near St. Petersburg, closed after decades of decline. Though about fifty people attended the final service, the church had dwindled to only nineteen regular attenders. As one elderly member observed, "If we had this many people every Sunday, we wouldn't be closing."[9]

The church was one of the longest-standing institutions in the city, but financial realities finally caught up to them. The decline had begun in the 1970s, and the neighborhood church slowly dwindled toward death over the next fifty years.

"When we lost the youth, we never got them back," the church's longest-standing member said. "As older members died, they didn't get replaced."[10]

A local reporter attended the final service and wrote an article giving a tender account of the church's final day. The article revealed what the remaining church members believed was their undoing. The larger, contemporary churches had more to offer. Families who sent their kids to an elementary school that rented part of the facility already had their own churches. The church got too old. People didn't like the ministries they offered.

What wasn't reported in the article was a heart for evangelism, a passion for the neighborhood, or a willingness to change. You can feel the poor self-image of the church in the article. The quotes from members reek of resignation. The reporter's description of the church says a lot: "That morning, there was no trace of the spare Bibles, the crockpots or the unused tins of decaffeinated coffee that littered the hallway earlier that week. The debris of 75 years' worth of Sundays had been cleared out just in time."[11]

It doesn't have to be this way. Start clearing out the debris! Why wait to clean up the church for the funeral? Believing the myths conforms you to the stereotypes. In Haggai, the foundation of the Temple was still there beneath the rubble. God worked when the people started cleaning up the mess and preparing for the future.

The challenges are real, but you don't have to buy in to the myths of the neighborhood church. You don't have to resign yourself to failure. It's time to start a movement that flips the script. The neighborhood church is primed for a surprising comeback.

6

The Current Challenges
of Neighborhood Churches

"I DON'T LIKE any of the changes, but people are accepting Jesus, so I guess I'll keep my mouth shut."

These words were spoken by the elderly matriarch of a midsize neighborhood church in a suburban city near the Front Range of the Rocky Mountains. The words themselves were hard enough to hear, but her tone was what took me aback. She understood the importance of evangelism, but her heart lacked a passion for people.

"I helped start this church over fifty years ago, and we made it feel like home," she said. She had grown up in the Deep South, before a job offer in the early 1970s brought her out West. The church had started as a refuge for Southern transplants who wanted church to be the way it was back home. The strategy worked well for about twenty years. As surrounding suburbs popped up in the 1970s, 1980s, and into the 1990s, the church grew to more than three hundred in weekly attendance. But as with many neighborhoods, transitions occurred, and the area's demographics changed. When the church did not change in response, a gradual decline began.

About four years ago, the church's pastor started making some needed shifts in programming, worship style, and polity. But the most significant change was to the church's culture. What was once a "come here if you fit in" mentality became "we will meet you where you are." Evangelism and outreach were placed at the forefront of every ministry in the church. As a result, for the first time in years the church began to grow.

At first, the existing members loved the influx of new people. The worship center was full on Sunday mornings, and the children's ministry tripled. After a couple of years, some of the new people began to serve in leadership roles. That's when the tension started to build. The problems seemed to come out of nowhere. Longtime members appeared happy about the growth one day and were up in arms the next. This shift in mentality is not uncommon in growing, smaller churches. From a sociological standpoint, it's all about power. A decades-old church growth idea called "the berry bucket theory" helps provide some perspective for pastors who come into existing churches.[1]

Old berries represent people who were in the church before the pastor arrived. New berries represent people who come to the church after the pastor. On the pastor's first day, the old berry bucket is as full as it will ever be. Over time, it will lose berries as people move away, change churches, or die. Meanwhile, the new berry bucket begins to fill up as new people move into the neighborhood, families expand, and transfer growth occurs.[2]

When the new bucket has about the same number of berries as the old bucket, tensions start to build; the old berries perceive that their power is slipping away. In most churches, this dynamic takes about three or four years to surface. Once equilibrium is reached, the old berries will act to retain organizational power. Sometimes there is a catalyst moment, such as a business meeting vote that doesn't go the way the old berries anticipated. In a matter of days, their love of growth turns into a disdain for new people. Does this problem happen in every church? No, but it's not uncommon.

Many neighborhood churches are simply not ready for change. They wouldn't know what to do if a hundred guests showed up one Sunday. They have an entrenched mindset. Many neighborhood churches don't think about growth. Some probably don't even want growth. They remain small not because of a lack of opportunity but because of a lack of effort.

While I believe a comeback is just over the horizon, the church must address specific challenges. In the next chapter, I will address how to lead change in a neighborhood church. In chapter 8, I will offer some tangible steps for moving toward health and growth. For now, let's examine the challenges. When we understand the obstacles, it's easier to figure out how to navigate past them.

Systems and Structures Built for Maintenance, Not Growth

The Front Range church had gone into maintenance mode. Because the church had started as a place for transplanted Southerners to feel at home, they developed programs that maintained the culture and met the expectations of their congregants. For several years, enough babies were born into the church to offset the number of older folks who passed away. Unfortunately, this equilibrium created a deep complacency in the church. Eventually, the culture they created caught up to them, and equilibrium shifted subtly into a gradual decline. No one felt it at first. But once the congregation dipped below one hundred, people started waking up to the reality of the church's regression.

"I must admit," the matriarch commented, "we were dying." The initial reaction of the old berries was to try harder with their current programs. They blamed the younger generation for abandoning the church. In reality, people were not abandoning the church but graduating from it. The group of high school seniors got smaller and smaller each year. Graduation Sunday was no longer necessary, not because families had left, but because the church was not reaching anyone new. When the last large group of children reached maturity, there was not another group behind them. The outdated programs no longer resonated with families. As in many struggling churches, the congregation made programs an end rather than a means.

The real sticking point was the drama ministry. The older generations remembered the large-scale productions from previous decades. Twice a year, the children and students would perform on a Sunday morning. These productions were gospel-centric and done with excellence. But for whatever reason, the number of young people involved dwindled as many of the leaders got older. People complained about the quality of the performances. The old berries—who no longer volunteered in the children's or student ministries—pushed the church to keep the old programs running, even though younger families wanted something different. The small number of remaining families was enough to justify the maintenance of the old programs, but the productions became a source of disappointment rather than inspiration. When the new pastor canceled the program and started making changes, he took a lot of heat, even though hardly anyone was involved anymore. Maintenance mode is dangerous because the ideals of the past overrule plans for the future.

Levels of Nostalgia Are Higher than Passion for Mission

Many people experience nostalgia. A certain song plays and takes you back. You drive by the old downtown movie theater that now houses a dance company. You visit your childhood home. The feeling of nostalgia is normal and expected. The church, however, will not function well when feelings of nostalgia overwhelm a passion for God's mission in the world today.

In the book of Ezra, a group of people complain during the rebuilding of the Temple. They lament how the new structure will be nothing compared to Solomon's Temple. At the time of their complaint, the foundation had just been restored. They started complaining at the very beginning of the project! Their nostalgia for a previous era undermined their passion for the task at hand.

The mission of the church is never in the past. If you love the past more than the future, you are outside the will of God. Show me a church that loves the past more than the future, and I will show you a disobedient church. Here's why: God doesn't save anyone in the past, but he can save people now and he will save people in the future. Nostalgia is not always bad. Fond memories can prompt us to act today. Nostalgia becomes a problem when we long for the past more than we anticipate God's work in the future. Nostalgia produces paralysis. Overly nostalgic churches become apathetic to God's active Kingdom work.

"When my grandson was baptized, it changed my perspective," the church matriarch continued. "I will never understand why our long-standing traditions can't work today. But my grandson would not still be in the church without the changes we made."

"She still complains," the pastor told me. "A lot. But the venom is gone. The toxicity is no longer present in the church. We're moving forward, and our brightest days are ahead of us."

Landmarks and Memorials Are More Important than the Next Generation

"Sam, someone ran over the historical marker at the church."

I'll never forget that phone call. The man chuckled a bit as he told me about the scene. Our building in Murray, Kentucky, was on the National Register of Historic Places, and many people in the church had a sense of pride about it.[3] I forget the details of how it occurred, but I knew I would field questions the following Sunday morning. Thankfully, the church took it in stride. The sign was replaced, and the history remained intact.

Along with our memorial marker, we had some historic landmarks. A landmark can be any widely recognizable physical feature. In a church building, a landmark could be anything from the architectural features of the building to the stained glass windows, hand-carved pews, steeple, pulpit, or bells in the belfry. In our case, it was the stained glass windows, which had fallen into disrepair and needed to be replaced. Our church went through a process of selecting new windows and finding a competent installer, but then the town historical society informed us that we were not allowed to replace the windows.

"Pieces are falling out," we told them at a city council meeting. "It's a safety hazard."

The city would not budge. Not only were we on the National Register, but we were also in a historic overlay district, which is designed to preserve the historic character of a neighborhood. Over the next several months, we spent considerable time trying to get permission to change the windows. They eventually relented when we agreed to make the new windows look exactly like the old ones. By then, local and national media outlets were asking to interview me about church and state issues. The community wanted the church to look the same way it had looked in the past. Not that we were opposed to that, but we wanted to focus on the present and win the next generation for Christ. Both agendas finally converged, but it took a lot of energy and created a lot of friction.

In unhealthy neighborhood churches, maintaining landmarks and memorials becomes the priority and focus of the church. "To be frank," writes Mark Clifton, "it is easier to spend time and money fixing a building than doing the hard work to become an indispensable part of the fabric of the community."[4] In declining churches, preserving the past is more important than reaching future generations. The hallways are empty of children but filled with portraits of previous pastors. Trophy cases display historical accomplishments, but the next generation is not there for the passing of the baton of ministry. Struggling churches will have difficulty distinguishing between what is timeless (God's mission) and what is temporary (programs, landmarks, even buildings).[5] In extreme cases, the community knows the neighborhood church only for its landmarks. Sometimes, these precious landmarks are what keep people at a distance. They're reluctant to come inside, as if the church building is a national memorial where you're not supposed to lean over the ropes or touch the exhibits. But a church is not a historical display in the middle of a neighborhood; the church campus should be the locus of community interaction.

The Church No Longer Reflects or Respects the Neighborhood

"I didn't grow up this way," the matriarch of the Front Range church said, "but my upbringing wasn't exactly right." She described how she struggled seeing interracial couples in the church. God was reshaping her, and the impact was felt among her peers. They, too, were beginning to realize that churches didn't need to be segregated, and families could be a blend of colors. As in many other parts of the United States, the church's neighborhood was changing, becoming more multiethnic. The church should reflect the neighborhood for the simple reason that they are reaching the neighbors.

Dying churches refuse to adapt to the changing community. Instead, they become like fortresses, keeping the current crowd safe from outsiders.[6] Your church will never reflect the neighborhood if you don't respect your neighbors. Sometimes churches deride the ethnic or socioeconomic shifts in their neighborhoods. Far too often, churches choose to relocate to a similar demographic rather than assimilate a changing demographic.

This mode of thinking was prevalent during the height of the church growth movement, when many leaders advocated the *homogeneous unit principle*—the idea that "people like to become Christians without crossing racial, linguistic, or class barriers. . . . They prefer to join churches whose members look, talk, and act like themselves."[7]

Donald McGavran, whose definition of the homogeneous unit principle is quoted here, gave an interesting example focusing on class differences among whites, which may help us look beyond the racial and ethnic tensions in our current society.

> In Denver, Colorado, a Presbyterian congregation was declining because its members were moving out to the suburbs. The new whites moving into that part of the city did not join this congregation in any but the smallest numbers. The class barrier (which would have been vehemently denied by the congregation), while not high, was there. It was inconspicuous but powerful.

Though many leaders of the church growth movement warned against ethnocentrism and racism, some favored a more segregated church. The homogeneous unit principle evolved to become a means of rationalizing why churches didn't necessarily need to assimilate people across ethnicities. Proposals for dealing with African Americans moving into white neighborhoods called for white churches to move out to the suburbs rather than encouraging them to work to become heterogeneous in the city. In an odd twist, calls to break the comfort of tradition stood side by side with rationalizations for not becoming *too* uncomfortable by reaching out to people of different backgrounds.

In recent years, church growth experts are more likely to support heterogeneous congregations, based on the idea that the best and most authentic evangelism is one that seeks to bridge all divides, including culture, ethnicity, and socioeconomics. As the American landscape becomes more multicultural, churches should reflect this mosaic in their congregations. The church that respects their neighbors will be the one that reflects the neighborhood.

The Megachurch Down the Road Is . . . Fading?

This topic surfaces in almost every consultation or interview we do. People in smaller churches believe that megachurches have taken— or "stolen" as they often say—their families. The matriarch in our interview certainly thought so. She named almost a dozen families that had left her church to attend the megachurch in their area. Some truth exists in these fears. A significant percentage of growth in large churches occurs because of transfer growth.[8] With low birth rates in the United States, most churches are not growing through larger families. Sadly, conversion growth in churches is rare, as few believers are actively engaged in the ministry of evangelism.

Megachurches receive more media attention than smaller churches. Their physical campuses can dominate their surrounding community. Megachurch pastors tend to have charisma, and their churches can offer a wide variety of programs appealing to a broad base of people. Megachurches also have a large gravitational pull. More people tend to drift toward these churches than to smaller congregations. Once a church reaches two thousand in weekly attendance, its sheer size becomes a self-generating attraction.[9] Massive facilities, a sprawling campus, and numerous attendees give these large congregations more prominence than other churches. One can understand why a smaller church would feel threatened by the megachurch down the road. But this threat is more perception than reality.

The megachurch movement is beginning to wane. The number of megachurches increased exponentially in the 1980s and 1990s, but long about 2010 this exponential growth stalled. The megachurch movement reached an inflection point with about 1,600 megachurches in the United States.[10] Over the next ten years, up to the pandemic of 2020, the number of megachurches dropped to about 1,200.[11] New worship spaces were also significantly smaller—about 20 percent on average—during the same time frame.[12] The pandemic then caused many megachurches to drop below 2,000 in average weekly attendance. In a 2022 *Christianity Today* article, leaders of a megachurch that for various reasons has seen a 57 percent decline in attendance said, "In our informal network with other large churches, we know of only two churches experiencing attendance and engagement beyond 60 percent of their pre-Covid numbers, with many around 50 percent."[13] If this anecdotal evidence holds true, the number of megachurches in the United States will be half of what it was before the pandemic.

Though it is difficult to estimate precisely how many megachurches remain in the United States, it's safe to assume the large growth curves of the 1980s and 1990s are a thing of the past. The movement was essentially a product of the Baby Boomer generation. These churches grew as the Baby Boomers came of age.

The Boomers are now aging out, and the megachurches are fading along with them. Will megachurches disappear? I believe there will always be healthy megachurches across the nation, but the phenomenon of megachurch growth is no longer in ascendency. Some other model must now take the lead.

The stigma of small is fading. People want to connect locally and within their neighborhoods. Churches with worship space for 200 to 600 are now ideal. Filling the giant rooms of megachurches is getting harder and harder. Neighborhood churches have a large-scale opportunity in front of them. Your neighbors, however, will not flock to your church just because you are smaller. If megachurches in your area are declining, that doesn't mean your church will benefit from their losses. Frankly, we should never place our hopes of growth on the decline of another church. Because few churches are doing the work of evangelism, those that begin are likely to experience fruit. God is saving people and will continue to save people. He will use the churches that are obedient. Your neighborhood church can make a comeback. Get excited about the transition!

Your Church Can Make the Transition to Better Health

The challenges in this chapter are real. I've addressed them not to bring you down but to help you recognize the obstacles. Once you see the obstacles, you can create pathways through them and around them. The most successful church turnarounds are the ones more focused on consistency and direction than speed.[14] You can transition your church. Better health is not a dream. I believe neighborhood churches can transition from remembering the past to being inspired about the future. Neighborhood churches can transition from glory days to God's glory. Neighborhood churches can transition from yesterday's legacy to today's mission. How can you lead this change? The next chapter will help you get started.

7

Leading Change in the Neighborhood Church

I'VE MADE A LOT OF MISTAKES as a pastor. One of the more memorable ones involved a complaint about worship. My wife had led the worship service on a Sunday many years ago, and someone did not like her song selection. After the service, the upset member made her grievance known (loudly) in the foyer for all to hear.

"That wasn't real worship! How terrible!" She then added a few other choice comments about my wife.

I responded, "There are plenty of dead churches in this town who would welcome another corpse if you don't like it here."

She never returned. I did not help her spiritually. My unpastoral response pushed her away from being a true worshiper. She was selfish, and I was callous. Two negatives did not make a positive.

The upset member wanted the status quo. I was leading change. The clash was inevitable, but it didn't have to culminate in a heated exchange.

The seminal work on leading change in the church was written in 1972 by Lyle Schaller. Though it's more than fifty years old, *The Change Agent* is still worth a careful, slow read. Among Schaller's many great insights is the idea that a reformer of the church must know the organization better than those who desire to control it.[1] For change to occur, a neighborhood church must get out of the power run cycle—whether that power resides with the pastor, several families, or another group of influencers. These competing power interests often create unnecessary conflict. Rather than working together, people in the church become suspicious of the motives of others.

When I responded sharply to the woman who had insulted my wife, I didn't take the time to ask a simple question: *Who is she?* I later learned she was one of the church matriarchs and an influential community leader with a long history of philanthropy. What might have happened if I had built a bridge instead of responding with the same animosity she had directed at me? I will never know.

As a pastor, you will hear these words at some point: "This is the way we do things. It's the way it's always been done." People say this for a reason. They prefer the status quo. Such is the case in many areas of life, not just the church. Talk to a baseball purist, and he or she will likely mention that the latest changes in Major League Baseball are ruining the game. Listen to someone who grew up in a small town, and he or she will lament how encroaching development is taking away the town's charm. Audiophiles have argued for decades that music sounds better recorded on vinyl than in any other format.

You cannot lead change until you understand why some people resist it. Why does the baseball purist prefer the old rules? What is it about new development that may hurt a small town? Maybe music does sound better on vinyl. But how will you know unless you listen to it?

The stakes are much higher in the church. Baseball and music are wonderful forms of entertainment and art, but the mission of God has eternal consequences. If a church is in decline, then something must change. But you cannot lead change unless you know the church better than those who desire to control it. I will start by unpacking the dangers of the status quo.

Why the Status Quo Is So Tempting. . . and Dangerous

Ronald Reagan once stated, "Status quo, you know, that is Latin for 'the mess we're in.'"[2] Most neighborhood churches that clamor for the status quo are messes. You don't often hear of a healthy church championing the status quo. Visionary leaders don't compel others to stay the same.

Of course, not everything in a church—even an unhealthy one—needs to change. The status quo is not necessarily the enemy. Status quo simply refers to the existing state of affairs. Sometimes the status quo is healthy. If daily exercise is status quo for you, then you're disciplined. Healthy habits don't need to be changed.

The problem with the status quo in many churches is that the churches aren't healthy—and every church could be healthier. Satisfaction with the status quo is the same as believing you've arrived. Nobody reaches glorification on this earth, and the last time I checked, billions still need to hear the gospel. Status quo churches will never reach the nations. Maintaining status quo is tempting—and dangerous.

Every church should seek to reach more people and go to more places. Status quo opposes more. The temptation of maintaining status quo is that you can be satisfied with the church's current missions footprint. The danger is that people may not hear the gospel because we were the ones who were supposed to go and reach them, but we settled for status quo. Most people pushing for status quo want to stay put, but I'm not aware of a biblical mandate that says, "Just stay put."

The stagnation of status quo is highly contagious. Have you ever been part of a meeting where a lot of effort was exerted for no gain? Then someone speaks up and says, "Let's wrap this up and reconvene later." And everyone quickly agrees. It's easy to convince people to stay the same. It's harder to get them to change. And that's why too many church meetings end with few, if any, action items.

Status quo discourages risk. One of the great temptations of leadership is to build a culture of maintaining status quo. When people don't expect big things, even little things seem like grand accomplishments. Church leaders can feel quite good about themselves when everyone congratulates them on the little accomplishments. It's easy to neglect big things when you receive a steady stream of praise for the little things. The danger in status quo churches is missing out on the grand rewards that come with taking risks for the Kingdom.

Status quo encourages complacency. If everyone is happy with the way things are, why upset the apple cart? The status quo is focused entirely inward, on people who are already in the church body, without considering those who still need to be reached.

Status quo leaves people unprepared for disruption. The struggle between good and evil will play out in your congregation. It's inevitable—somehow, some way, and at some point, there will be disruption, even if you work hard to prevent it. Status quo leaders leave their people unprepared for the inevitable upheaval. Far better to build a culture that expects disruptions, because they will happen.

"Don't move."

"Stay the same."

"No need to grow."

"We're content with the people we have."

Those statements don't make for a compelling vision. But the status quo doesn't make such bold declarations. It's more subtle. Don't be lured by this temptation. Its hook is dangerous and sneaky. Many neighborhood churches are stuck in a culture of complacency. The status quo acts as blinders, keeping the people from seeing the obvious. Churches lean into this because it represents safety—the known, the consistent, and the predictable. When you lead people away from their comfort zone and out into the neighborhood, you're asking them to become vulnerable by engaging in an unknown world that could present dangers.[3] Leading change is challenging when people are satisfied with the status quo, but there are some practical ways to start moving out of the rut.[4]

Two Often-Missed Factors That Can Stall Change Efforts

Some volatile congregations are a few steps away from insolvency, but most established neighborhood churches tend to be more stable. Though stability can become the rut where churches get stuck, it's also a blessing. Unlike many church plants, established churches have an existing revenue stream and a known location. One church plant renamed itself "Church on the Move" because they had to switch locations so often at the beginning of their history. Church planters dream about having an established location with a usable facility. Most neighborhood churches also have rhythms and patterns of programming with a set of volunteers already in place. These forms of stability can create ruts and an entrenched mentality, but don't overlook the fact that at least you have a road to drive on.

Don't Lose Your Rhythm

Rhythms are weekly (sometimes monthly) patterns of the people in your church. The weekly rhythm of my church includes gathering together on Sunday mornings and Wednesday evenings. Even something mundane, like a meeting, can become part of the rhythm. I've often heard church leaders lament, "We don't need to meet for the sake of meeting." That makes sense. But what if meetings are part of the natural rhythm of your church? Rather than disrupting the natural patterns in your church, use them! Give them a purpose. It's much easier to go with the flow and steer people in that flow than to get everyone into an entirely new pattern.

"My first initiative is to cancel the Christmas pageant," the new lead pastor told me. I winced internally. The pageant had indeed become a tail wagging the dog. It took up a chunk of the budget and required everyone in the church to be all-hands-on-deck starting in July. The energy of the church would be better spent in other areas. But the neighborhood loved the program, and many church members didn't see why the pageant was a problem. Canceling the program would only confuse the community and make the church members angry.

The church had a rhythm. After the spring semester of classes, everyone began preparing for the Christmas pageant. A group wrote the script. Others helped build the props for the stage. Costumes were designed. The children's programming shifted to teach the songs. Canceling the program without a viable replacement would be a disaster. Thankfully, the pastor realized his error and didn't make this change his first initiative. Instead, he accepted the director's invitation to play the lead role. Then he reprised the role the following year. Eventually, he began to work with the church on ways to preserve the pageant but without it encroaching on the weekly programming for half the year. Because the church knew he was invested in the pageant, they trusted him enough to listen to his suggestions.

"We've all been doing this for decades," one older member said, "and I think we could use a change." The church revamped the pageant in a way that didn't require everyone's involvement starting in the summer. As a result, they had time to create a vibrant children's church ministry and choir. People who had devoted their talents to the Christmas production now put them to use in equipping the next generation for worship. More families started attending the church as a result.

"Our family has attended your pageant in the past. It's excellent!" one new attender remarked. "Now you're offering this program for our kids, and I think we've found our church home." If the pastor had killed the pageant without consideration for the existing rhythms of the church, the move would have been disastrous. Instead, he used the rhythm to craft a better alternative over time. The road (the scheduling rhythm) was a good one. What was needed was a little time to get the church out of the rut that ran down the middle.

Don't Crumble Your Structure

"We've got to do something about our governance," the executive pastor said. "We're stuck in our structure." He shared how his church had more than twenty standing committees.

"The flower committee has nine members!" he laughed. "We have a committee on committees *and* a nominating committee. I'm not even sure about the difference."

You could tell he was tired of dealing with the morass of assembling so many people to get things done. He had a point. It's hard to implement a cohesive vision when the church's decision-making process is diluted by two dozen committees.

"I've got a meeting with my bylaws committee. My proposal is to reduce the number of committees to four."

His proposed structure was excellent. A personnel committee would deal with staff issues. The stewardship committee would handle the facility and finances. A missions committee would help with local outreach and cross-cultural trips. Then a nominating committee would select members for the other three committees.

"Will the other committee members view this move as a power grab?" I asked.

He had not considered that possibility. His motives were pure. His perspective was one of organizational structure rather than individual personalities.

"How often do the committees meet?"

"About ten times a year," he answered.

"How many committees are truly active?"

"Probably ten."

"With nine on each committee, that means you have ninety people in your church volunteering regularly."

He nodded.

"Rather than dismantling the whole system, why not tweak the existing structure in a more fluid way?"

You could see the wheels begin to turn. In his frustration, he had assumed the only option was to create an entirely new structure. But he quickly discovered that the church was far more open to simply adjusting the current structure. Over the course of a year, they dissolved committees that were in the bylaws but not active. Then they combined several committees with compatible or overlapping responsibilities. Eventually, they ended up with four committees that met quarterly and two that met monthly. The new structure wasn't ideal in the executive pastor's mind, but it enabled him to accomplish most of his agenda without alienating anyone.

Had he crumbled the entire structure, he likely would have lost most of his volunteer base and pushed away his best leaders.

Changing the Status Quo: The Top Priority of Culture

I have two shelves of books about leading change in the church. Classics like *Advanced Strategic Planning* demonstrate how to create new and sustainable growth curves.[5] Other books, such as *Leading Congregational Change,* give practical guidance on transforming churches through systems thinking.[6] The problem is that few books, if any, address leading cultural change from the perspective of a neighborhood church. In this chapter, my purpose is to build on the principles found in other works rather than repeat them.

An elusive question remains: *What does cultural change look like in a neighborhood church?* Growth models and systems are critical to change efforts, but they don't work without a corresponding culture shift in the church. Cultural change is deeper than implementing new systems; cultural change requires a shift in values, priorities, and perceptions.

Start Here: The Most Revealing Question to Ask Your Church

Leaders who implement cultural change ask a lot of questions. Who are the influencers? How many are supporters? Who stirs up discontent among the congregation? What has the church valued historically? How has the church made decisions in the past few years? How does the community view the church? How does the church view the neighborhood?

When I do a consultation through Church Answers, I have to ask a lot of questions. Over the years, I've refined the types of questions I ask and the way I ask them. Some questions don't elicit much of a response. Others cause people to pause and think. Then there are questions that get people talking. Some of the best learning experiences for leaders are when they ask a good question and then *listen*. After twenty years of researching churches, I've found that one question seems to get people talking more than any other: "What gets your church most excited?" or, "What gets you most excited about your church?"

The question isn't threatening, because it gives people a chance to offer a positive answer. At the same time, it narrows potential responses to the most exciting issues. It funnels a larger response into a single reply.

The answer reveals *passion*. The word *exciting* implies enthusiasm. When people talk about what gets them excited, we get an idea of what drives their passion. I've heard a wide range of answers—from theology to programs to buildings to missions to preaching. Rarely are people negative about their passions, so their answers reveal what they feel is most positive about their church.

The answer reveals *priorities*. What is most exciting is often considered most important. When we're passionate about something, we usually elevate it above other things.

The answer reveals *perspective*. Is the church's excitement rooted in the past, present, or future? Excitement about the past usually points to a lack of excitement about the present. On the other hand, excitement about the future could indicate that the person sees the church moving in a positive direction or is hopeful things will change soon.

The answer reveals *personality*. Every church has a different personality. Some churches are more extroverted, and they see new people as exciting. Some churches are more thoughtful, and members get excited about caring for others. Some churches are generous, and there is excitement around giving to God's Kingdom. The locus of excitement in a church often reflects the church's personality.

One question cannot uncover every important aspect of a church. But asking people what gets them excited reveals a lot of information in a nonthreatening way. It's one of the more common questions I ask in my consultations—and also in my own church. I enjoy hearing different perspectives in what is almost always a pleasant and positive context.

Maintain a Presence in the Neighborhood

One of the best ways to change a culture is through presence. When we move from one location to another, we encounter a change in perspective prompted by our new surroundings. Cross-cultural missionaries experience this shift in dramatic ways. But we can also experience a cultural change simply by leaving the church campus and serving in the neighborhood. Far too often, the culture of a church is wholly detached from the culture of the community. A church may develop a strong local influence when the congregants establish a consistent presence among their neighbors.

There are several ways to weave the church into the fabric of the community. Informally, we can hang out with the neighbors. Go where they are. More formally, we can adopt a local school. Start a fostering ministry. Partner with other ministries and civic organizations. Culture changes when our presence changes. Lead your church to be physically present in your neighborhood, and you will see an insular culture change to a more outwardly focused mindset.

Celebrate with the Neighborhood

As humans, we tend to celebrate what we value. Whatever a church celebrates regularly will inevitably become rooted in the culture of the congregation. A church can celebrate any number of milestones, people, or anniversaries. Recognizing these things isn't necessarily wrong. Churches that celebrate the fruits of evangelism, however, tend to have a culture that produces more passion for reaching others. Celebrate inwardly, and your church will have an inward culture. Celebrate outwardly, and your church will have more of an outward focus.

One of the best ways to demonstrate Christian joy is by showing unbelievers and the unchurched how a fellowship of Christ-followers celebrates. First, don't party behind closed doors. When your church has a large celebration, let the community know and invite them to participate. Second, find ways to celebrate with the community. Some people will never come to a church, free food or not. The church, however, can go to community celebrations. Learn about community-wide events, such as festivals, shows, and fairs. Establish a presence there. Work with event organizers and ask about their biggest needs. Offer to serve.

Don't just throw a big party without some measure of planning and organization. Always assume that unaffiliated people will be present at church celebrations. Clearly explain the purpose and significance of the celebration. Take time to share the gospel. Have a team in place to follow up with anyone interested in knowing more about Jesus or the church.

Do it well. Few people enjoy a half-baked celebration. Unbelievers and the unchurched are less likely to experience the joy of Christ at a ho-hum church event. The only way to multiply a culture of evangelistic celebration is to celebrate with excellence. Live lives that exemplify Christ and celebrate his life in memorable ways.

By design, celebrations focus on the moment at hand or on a past event. However, they are also leading indicators of where a church is going. Celebrations help form culture. When you examine what a congregation celebrates, you will gain insight into the culture of that church.

Pray for the Neighborhood

A church's prayer list reveals the church's priorities. Fill your prayer list with requests from the neighborhood. Ask the neighbors how you can pray for them. When you create a regular pattern of praying for the neighbors, it's impossible not to think about them. They become a priority. Positive cultural change will not occur in the church apart from prayer. There is an unmistakable connection between dependent prayer and effective mission.[7] If you don't pray through cultural change, you will rely on your own abilities instead of God's sovereignty. Cultural change without prayer is dangerous because you won't know whether God is in the change.

Tailor Ministries to the Neighborhood

God sovereignly placed your church in your neighborhood with the specific focus of reaching and serving the neighbors. The neighborhood does not exist for the church; the church exists for the neighborhood. Therefore, the church's ministries should reflect the community's needs. Take a look at your operating budget. What percentage of resources is dedicated to the neighborhood? What portion of resources is dedicated to reaching the nations? And how much is used for internal purposes?

At Church Answers, in our work with healthy neighborhood churches nationwide, we have found that around 25 percent of the operating budget will be earmarked for local ministry and missions. Each ministry should have a portion of the budget specified for serving the neighbors. The children's ministry should host events for the neighborhood kids. The missions budget may include funds to serve foster families in the area. The worship ministry should sing in nursing homes, create music camps for teenagers, and go Christmas caroling, among other outreach ministries. The first impressions ministry should have funds to make gift bags for the neighbors. Go door-to-door and deliver these gifts to twenty-five neighbors a month. These efforts will dramatically shift the culture of your church over time.

Share the Church Facility with the Neighborhood

As I mentioned in the first chapter, when pastors do not lead the church to serve the community, the congregants will respond with either apathy or antagonism. When you stop listening to the neighbors, you stop caring for the neighbors. When you stop caring for the neighbors, they can come to be seen as the enemy. Apathetic churches become cultural islands detached from the neighborhood. Angry churches will go on the attack against the neighborhood.

One of the best ways to prevent apathy and antagonism is to share space with your neighbors. An open church campus is an invitation to a healthier relationship between church and community. A healthy neighborhood church will view their campus as a shared resource. Build a playground and let the neighborhood children play there. Take down the chains closing off the parking lot. Install picnic benches under trees for the neighbors to congregate and eat. Of course, you must take into consideration issues of liability and security. But those concerns are not insurmountable. Does your church culture default to an open campus model or a closed campus model? When you limit the church facility to members only and shut out the neighbors, you send a message to everyone that guests are not welcome. A healthy church culture will find ways to open the campus to the neighbors.

Getting Started: You Only Need Two or Three

Why do many pastors and church leaders start leading the process of change with new structures, systems, and marketing? These items are more technical in nature and don't require a cultural shift. For example, you can rewrite the bylaws and call for a church vote without a culture shift. The issue is whether the church will embrace the change as part of its identity, which points to a broader cultural acceptance.

Though technical changes can be the work of a single leader, cultural change typically requires a group. However, cultural change doesn't require the up-front agreement of the entire church. You can initiate cultural change without involving everyone. It takes only two or three key influencers or passionate people to start the process.

Imagine the impact if three families in the church decide to focus on outreach and evangelism. What if each of these three families pulled in three other families? Now you have a dozen families excited about the direction of the church. And because nine of those families were brought in through outreach, those activities are normative for them.

Could twelve families working together begin to shift the culture of the church? In most churches, yes. Think about how many struggling churches are controlled by two, three, or four families. The same can be true for revitalized neighborhood churches. Two, three, or four families with a positive influence can turn the tide of the culture.

Don't be discouraged if most of your church isn't ready to embrace cultural changes. These shifts occur over time. But the process can begin now with a small group. In the next chapter, I will describe practical ways you can start to reach your neighbors. Get your team together. Even if at first you are not many in number, your impact can help change the direction of your entire church.

8

Effective Strategies to Reach the Neighbors

HEALTHY THINGS GROW. Perhaps you have heard a version of this phrase in connection with church growth principles. I think most people mean well when they use the phrase. However, I've heard it used to denigrate smaller, struggling churches. Some have used it to justify some questionable practices in large, rapidly expanding churches. Yet, the spirit of the saying is true. Healthy things do grow. The issue is one of pace, sustainability, and integrity.

The eastern hemlock is a slow-growing tree, adding about a foot of height each year. This slow, steady growth gives the tree several advantages, including durability and longevity. Most soils and odd slopes are not a problem for the eastern hemlock. They are hearty trees and can grow in various soils, terrain, and light. Their lifespan is also quite long—800 years or more—and they don't reach maturity until 250 to 300 years into their growth cycle.[1]

There is something to be said about the durability and longevity of slow and steady growth.

Weeds grow quickly. Their growth can choke out the growth of other, more desirable plants. Invasive species also grow, but their growth is in the wrong place. I hope the analogy is clear. The growth of the eastern hemlock is the better option. The steady growth of a neighborhood church can mean a durable and long-lived presence in the place where God has planted it. Churches should not be weeds, growing in a way that chokes out the neighborhood. Churches should not be an invasive species, with the neighborhood wishing they would go somewhere else. Even healthy growth doesn't happen continuously. Effective growth also includes seasons on the plateau.

The Pandemic Plateau and Moving Forward

There are times when a church attendance plateau is a victory. I believe many churches are in a season of stagnation, and it's not all bad. But first, a few caveats. Though stagnation is not the goal, a plateau can point to a future growth climb. Also, churches can be in denial about their decline. Leaders should never ignore problems.

When you're on a plateau, the first step is recognizing where you are. Unfortunately, churches and leaders can tend to lack self-awareness. Don't call a decline a plateau. The definition of a plateau is an extended season of neither growing nor declining. Be self-aware. You can't move forward if you don't know where you are.

At Church Answers, in the wake of the Covid-19 pandemic, we're seeing a trend of larger churches operating at about 60 percent pre-pandemic attendance and smaller churches operating at about 80 percent pre-pandemic attendance. Many churches are stuck right now at these levels and will likely remain there for the foreseeable future.

It's not all bad. Here's why. The Great Reshuffling is producing strong headwinds in our society. Millions of people every month are quitting their jobs. The news headlines scream of a "Great Resignation." People are making big changes *en masse*.[2] This phenomenon affects churches as well as neighborhoods and businesses. Churchgoers are moving to different places and considering other churches. I don't like the idea of church "resignation," so I use the term *reshuffling* instead. Whether it is spiritually healthy has yet to be determined. But the reshuffling is occurring. Steady attendance right now is a victory.

Attendance frequency rebounds slowly and gradually. One of the most common trends among churches today is decreasing attendance frequency. People are going to church less often. Attendance frequency measures how often a person goes to church. For example, an "active" member was once considered someone who came twice, or even three times a *week*. Today an active member is considered someone who comes at least twice a month.

Consider a church that has 400 people attending four out of four weeks. That church has an average weekly attendance of 400. Take the same church with the same people but lower the attendance frequency to two out of four weeks. That church's average weekly attendance is now 200. As attendance frequency declines, the congregation will feel smaller, even if the church is actually getting larger. Meanwhile, the people who are coming less often still email, call, and set up counseling appointments. They still ask the pastor to do funerals and weddings and come to the hospital.

Attendance stagnation could be the result of more people associating with the church but attending less often. Any gains in attendance frequency will occur slowly and through deliberate strategies to get people into a weekly rhythm of attendance. A pattern of more consistent attendance is what pastors should pursue with their congregants, but the effort will take months, if not years, to produce good results.

There is also a replacement issue with older congregants. I hope your church members live a long time! But the reality is that the older generations—the ones with more consistent church attendance patterns—are passing away. Over time, attendance stagnation means the church is gaining new people at a rate commensurate with those who are leaving or passing away. Growing younger as a church can create a plateau effect. It's always a good sign when the median age drops in a church. But in many cases, to retain attendance levels it takes two new people to replace one older person, because the older generations tend to be at church more often.

Whatever the reason for stagnation, it can be a frustrating problem. What are some ways that neighborhood churches can break out of the cycle of stagnation?

The Four Main Ways that Every Church Grows

Every person who joins your church is a unique story of God's grace. These individual stories are important and should be celebrated. From a statistical standpoint, however, there are four main types of church growth: *conversion*, *transfer*, *biological*, or *demographic*.

Conversion growth occurs when someone accepts Christ and is assimilated into the body as a new member and a new Christian. This growth is the preferred method as it points to evangelistic health and outreach efforts. The calling of the Great Commission requires every church to grow by making disciples who then make more disciples. Unfortunately, few churches grow in this way. Conversion growth has been declining for decades in the North American church.

Transfer growth occurs when an existing resident moves from one congregation to another within the same community. The megachurch phenomenon from the 1970s until about 2010 occurred in large part because of transfer growth. Bigger churches got bigger faster, but not because they figured out how to reach the unchurched.[3] Unfortunately, most "church growth" in the last several decades was merely the migration of people from one congregation to another.

Biological growth occurs when existing families in the church have children. These kids are raised in the church and become part of the body through their parents' connection. Obviously, we can't control how many kids will be born into a congregation, and not all those children will stay in their original church once they begin making decisions for themselves. But every church should be concerned with training up the next generation into mature (or maturing) believers who won't be inclined to leave the church after high school. Studies have shown that 70 percent of those who drop out do so between the ages of eighteen and twenty-two.[4] One-third of those will eventually return, usually once they start having children of their own, but if a church has a strong emphasis on discipleship during those formative years, maybe more young people will stay in the church and not drop out or wander away.

Demographic growth occurs when new residents arrive in the community and start looking for a church. The main difference between transfer and demographic growth is whether someone is new to the community. Transfer growth involves existing residents, whereas demographic growth involves new residents. Most new residents looking for a church will already be believers, but that may not be the case with everyone. Some new residents will seek a church because they are searching spiritually.

As you formulate a strategy for growth, your top priority should be conversion growth. Churches should try to minimize transfer growth. Exceptions include when someone's former church makes wholesale changes to doctrine or when someone is pushed out. Sometimes families decide to worship together and move their membership to the same church. And there are life-stage issues, such as when an adult son or daughter transfers to the church of an elderly parent. Not all transfer growth is bad, but churches should avoid transfer growth generated by people merely seeking their preferences. The focus for most churches should be conversion growth and demographic growth. Put most of your effort into reaching unbelievers and those who are new to the community.

Kick-Starting Outreach and Getting Off the Plateau

Mitch is an example of a pastor who recently discovered the potential impact of connecting with community leaders. He received a call from the superintendent of the large private school across from his church. Mitch had heard of the man's reputation as a militant atheist. So he did not have high hopes when the superintendent wanted to schedule a meeting.

"I assumed he wanted to chastise us for using their football parking lot on Sundays," Mitch told us. "After meeting with him, however, I was shocked to find that he didn't mind. He simply wanted to get to know me."

Mitch continued with a hint of guilt, "I assumed the worst about this guy based upon rumors I'd heard, yet now he and I have a great relationship." As a result of connecting with the superintendent, Mitch has a window into the needs of students and parents at a school where no one attends his church.

"They're right across the street, and I never thought about reaching out to them. I learned my lesson."

Mitch's situation is not unique. Church leaders ready to serve their neighbors may not know where to begin. Additionally, leaders unconnected to the church may not realize that the local church could meet their unique community needs. If a church is struggling to make an impact, the missing element might just be reaching out to other leaders. But before you make contact, consider four bits of insight.

Asking precedes understanding. Don't assume you know the most significant issues in the community. Instead, ask people to share their perspective. Asking helps clarify and prioritize known needs. Understanding the viewpoint of other leaders will also give you insight into how best to approach new community problems.

Connecting precedes service. Though churches do not need a local leader for every form of outreach, some of the best ideas will originate from leaders closely connected to the issues. Before beginning new service opportunities, contact local leaders and ask for their input.

Genuineness precedes relationships. True relationships are built on trust and authenticity—though not all community leaders will be receptive to even the most genuine intentions. If your goal is to politick when connecting with community leaders, your impact will greatly diminish. Don't have an agenda; simply meet with leaders and ask them how you can serve them.

Impact precedes receptiveness. At Church Answers, we hear stories all the time about how the unchurched are more willing to attend a service at a church that is making an impact in the local community. One of the complaints we hear from stagnant and declining churches is that people are not as receptive as they once were. But the more a church helps and cares for their community, the more receptive people will be to attending the church.

What are some practical ways to reach outward like Mitch did? Start at the front door.

THE SURPRISING RETURN OF THE NEIGHBORHOOD CHURCH

Know Your Neighbor: Meet Them at Their Front Door

"I have an idea," Jenny told me. "Let's get back to the basics and go to the front doors of our neighbors."

"You do know that's been done before," I responded.

"Yes, but this time we're going to bring fun gifts."

Jenny is one of the more creative minds on our team. She crafted a plan called the "Know Your Neighbor" campaign. The idea was simple. We would map out several homes around our church and bring the neighbors a small gift every month. The goal was for the gifts to be inexpensive, clever, and memorable. My favorite was the box of Lucky Charms we delivered on St. Patrick's Day with the note attached, "We're lucky to have you as neighbors." The deliveries created many opportunities to get to know the neighbors and invite them to church.

Another option is to utilize prayer walking as an outreach strategy. Prayer walking is a way for church members to gain first-hand knowledge of the neighborhood by observing the community in real time.[5] Prayer walking is an excellent way to increase your church's physical presence in the neighborhood. Spiritually, there is a lot of power when the church prays collectively on behalf of their neighbors.

No church is an island, and people are not designed to live in isolation. Unfortunately, far too many neighborhoods have become "*shelterhoods*," a collection of unconnected people living in proximity to each other.[6] Your neighbor's front door might as well be on Mars. We fall prey to Satan's lies about our lack of connection.

I just need to get through the day.

After things settle down, I'll get to know my neighbor.

Everyone lives this way.

We're all just busy right now.[7]

These lies become crushing blows to our work in God's Kingdom. They prevent us from taking the first steps to the front door of our neighbors. The best way to close the Sunday-to-Monday spiritual gap is to begin the process of getting to know your neighbor.[8]

Invite Your Neighbor: Ask Them to Come to Your Front Door

Charlie Moulton is a pastor you may not know, but he's one of the best. He shepherds Lakeshore City Church in Corona, California. It's a midsize church with a heart to reach the surrounding neighborhood. Almost half a million people live within a fifteen-minute drive of Charlie's church, which makes for a massive mission field. The hurdles are real. During the pandemic, they took over the lease from a church that closed and moved into their facility. The building is in a commercial part of the neighborhood without visible signage.

"People are not typically driving by and looking for a church anyway. Our guests are the ones who are invited."

Charlie makes a good point. Most guests end up at a specific church because of a personal invitation from a friend or family member. In fact, 82 percent of your neighbors are open to a personal invitation to church.[9] The problem is most churchgoers are not in the habit of regularly inviting others—at best inviting someone maybe once or twice a year. Almost one-third of churchgoers never invite anyone.[10] Most congregations do not have a culture of inviting.

Proper signage, a good location, a solid social media presence, clean facilities, and strategic marketing help the church gain visibility, but the top reason that guests will come is that they've been invited by their friends or family members.

What did Charlie's church do? They sent people out to the city parks.

"The parks here are popular, especially with our young moms," Charlie said. He described how they started small group meetings in the parks, and those became a way to interact with the community. Many of the guests at Lakeshore City first heard about the church through interactions at the local parks as their children had fun together on the playground. A storefront location with a lack of signage is not a problem for Lakeshore City. People come to the church because the members invite them.

Creating a culture of inviting guests to church can start with an emphasis Sunday. One of our more popular resources at Church Answers is *Invite Your One*, a step-by-step guide to having a successful outreach campaign.[11] The concept is simple. Focus on one Sunday on which everyone invites their friends and family to church. This special Sunday creates an excitement level and a way of holding people accountable to the task of inviting others.

Another way to create a culture of inviting others is to have churchwide fellowship activities on special days. For example, we have an Independence Day celebration on the Sunday closest to July 4th. There are water activities for the kids, hot dogs, and food trucks. A couple of years ago, we thought it would be a fun thing to do since July 4th is often one of our lowest attended Sundays. What happened amazed us. That Sunday was the highest attendance of our summer and one of the highest of the year! The reason was that people invited their friends. Several people from the neighborhood walked to church that day to join the fun. Some came back week after week, and a few recently joined the church.

Our Church Answers research shows that, in a healthy church, about 5 percent of your worshiping community will self-identify as guests. Though many guests are repeat attendees, here is the estimated number of guests per year for a church of 150:

(Avg. Weekly Worship Attendance) × (0.05) × (52)
150 × 0.05 × 52 = 390 guests per year!

Even a small movement toward creating an invite culture can bring in a substantial number of guests.

I believe many church leaders are guilty of overthinking growth strategies. You don't *need* fancy technology, a large budget, and over-the-top antics. The primary way that people come is through personal invitation. Regularly encourage your people to invite others, and guests will start arriving at your front door.

The Future Movements of Church Adoption and Church Fostering

No church should die. If God can save any person, he can save any church. Unfortunately, some churches will die. What was a looming crisis, perhaps unseen before the pandemic, is now on full display: declining church attendance. The pandemic accelerated and exacerbated existing problems. About one-third of regular churchgoers before the pandemic have not returned to in-person worship.[12] At this stage, it does not appear they will ever return. Church closures seem inevitable. But two new movements might be able to prevent this.

Some dying churches can be saved through internal revitalizations or external relaunches. Others will need to be fostered or adopted. Both church adoption and church fostering have the potential to spark revitalization. Church adoption refers to the process of blending two congregations into one family. Some refer to this process as a church merger. I prefer the term *adoption* because it pulls in biblical language. Most adoptions occur when a larger, healthier church assimilates another church into a multisite system. *Fostering* is a term connected to the adoption process in church revitalization. Church fostering happens when a healthier church sends people and resources to help a struggling church over a set time period, typically six months to a year. Church adoption is permanent. Church fostering is temporary.

These two movements excite me. When a neighborhood church closes permanently, the Kingdom of God loses an asset. Church adoption and fostering prevent closure. These two movements occur organically and are often rooted in relationships between pastors and church leaders. A struggling neighborhood church turns to a healthier church for help.

With fostering, both churches are typically located in the same community. The healthier church provides resources and people the other church doesn't have. These resources can include someone to preach, children's volunteers, curriculum, and facility maintenance, among others. Usually, these arrangements include a predetermined time frame with a specific focus. For example, a healthier church may help a church struggling with worship ministry by providing three musicians for a year, while training others to take on the responsibility. Some fostering arrangements may lead to adoption. If the fostered church cannot progress in a timely manner, the healthier church may adopt it. The fostering church, however, should not enter an arrangement with a secret agenda to take over the other church's campus. My church, West Bradenton, has entered three separate fostering arrangements with area neighborhood churches. They were challenging but rewarding. One of these churches became our Southside campus.

We started fostering this church right before the pandemic began. They did not have a pastor, so we sent them someone from our congregation to preach every week. We also sent people to help with worship. Southside approached us after a time of fostering and asked to become part of our family. We weren't ready, but there was no way we could turn them down! Now I understand God's timing. Southside would not have survived the pandemic on their own.

The Southside campus launched with fewer than ten volunteers and no budget funds. Our vision is to be a healthy neighborhood church and adopt other neighborhood churches into our family. We want to take churches of ten and twenty and help them become campuses of one hundred and two hundred. After our first adoption, we learned a few lessons.

Always perform formal due diligence. We had several layers of due diligence over the course of a year: leadership, doctrine, financial, facilities, and legal. During our legal due diligence, our lawyer uncovered that Southside had used variants of their church name on different legal documents. This discovery was significant because any documentation to formalize a merger needed the true name of the church. The most time-consuming and expensive part of our adoption was getting the legal name of the church right.

Many will not understand the vision for fostering or adopting at first, and that's okay. The church merger concept has existed for about twenty years, but it's still not a mainstream thought among parishioners. Using words like *adoption* is new. When I first proposed the vision of revitalizing churches through adoption, I knew people would need to see it in real time before they would fully understand it. Thankfully, my church was supportive. Likely, the multisite model via adoption will not become part of our culture until we open our third campus.

Wrong motives will crush you. Don't adopt a struggling church because you're looking for a quick-growth strategy. Adoption requires a deep love for the established church. Growing a healthy campus out of adoption may take years of work. Also, live preaching is preferable to video venues. Most adopted churches need the presence of a campus pastor, and it's preferable that this pastor be the one who preaches regularly. Our Southside campus simply would not have worked without a campus pastor.

Who you send is critical to long-term success. Church adoption requires both an entrepreneurial spirit and a patient mindset. The ideal volunteer will adapt to change quickly but also operate well in an established church setting. We asked our adopting team to commit to a year of direct participation. Many will stay longer. Others may find a permanent home in the new location. Don't send disgruntled members and hope they will thrive in a new place. Chances are they will disgruntle the people around them. Don't push people to go who would rather not go, regardless of how well you may think they would fit. Send the people who are most excited about the new work.

Bi-vocational or co-vocational campus pastors are the wave of the future. Our campus pastor is bi-vocational. He works at a local school and serves at our church. Many bi-vocational pastors would accept a full-time position if it were offered. A co-vocational pastor has a calling to both work in the marketplace and also serve the church. As more church adoptions occur, the need for both kinds of pastors will rise dramatically. Most church adoptions will require at least a part-time campus pastor.

Church adoption is messy. It's hard. It's confusing. It's frustrating. But great rewards come from complex challenges. I'm thrilled that we adopted Southside. They are part of our family now.

Locked in the Church When Jesus Is Locked Out

The book of Revelation contains seven letters to seven churches. Decades after Jesus ascended to heaven, churches began to form as he had commanded. They started ministering to their communities. Like today, some of these churches were healthy. Others were not. Then Jesus, through the apostle John, wrote to seven of these churches.

Jesus knew precisely what was happening in each church, just as he is acutely aware of what you are doing in *your* church. In Revelation, the church in Laodicea was known for being luke-warm. Laodicea was an important city on a well-traveled trade route. The people of Laodicea had a level of affluence, and their homes were known for being quite large. The city had a central-ized water system, with an aqueduct, and some homes even had an early form of indoor plumbing. Prominent people lived in Laodicea. Due to the city's wealth and its proximity to trade routes, Laodicea was a strategic location. If the gospel caught on there, it could potentially spread to many other places.

In Revelation 3, Jesus rebukes the church in Laodicea. He calls them lukewarm, like the water from their aqueduct. Cold water is good for drinking. Hot water is good for cleaning. Lukewarm water doesn't satisfy either purpose. Like one might spit out room-temperature coffee, Jesus tells the church he will spew them out if they are lukewarm in their faith.

Jesus then offers another rebuke, calling them "wretched and miserable and poor and blind and naked" (Revelation 3:17).

The people of the church did not see themselves the way Jesus describes them. They were rich and powerful. But Jesus reminds them they may be materially rich but spiritually poor. The church worshiped comfort over devotion to God's mission.

What did Jesus challenge them to do? He tells them to be diligent and turn from their indifference (Revelation 3:19). Then John records a famous image of Jesus. He is standing at the door knocking. Jesus is asking the church to open the door and let him in. In other words, the church has locked him out!

If you want to reach your neighbors, it will not happen if Jesus is locked out while you are playing church inside. The church—your church—must move outward with Jesus. Open the door. Let him back in.

9

Becoming a Neighborhood Church for the Nations

"You need to sit down," Janice said as she walked swiftly into my office.

Janice was our church's financial director, and with her big laugh and zest for life, she was more colorful than the stereotypical "bean counter." So when she approached my desk with such seriousness, I could tell she had something important to share.

"We started receiving dividend payments last month."

"I didn't know we owned stock."

My interruption prompted her to shush me.

"These payments were in the thousands of dollars."

Then reality hit me: "If the dividend payments are thousands of dollars, how much stock do we own?" My voice was elevated. "And where on earth did it come from? We don't show anything like this on our balance sheet!"

Janice now reverted to her more typical playful demeanor. "That's why I told you to sit down."

The explanation was complex. Our insurance provider had gone through a demutualization process, leaving us with shares in the new company. The only notice of this transition was the dividend payments. Janice had worked hard that week to determine the legitimacy of everything.

"This is real?"

"Yes, it is."

"How much stock do we own?"

"Well, it's at a fifty-two-week high right now. The current value is around $600,000. What do you want me to do?"

"Sell it!" I yelled with excitement.

The church was already in good financial shape. I knew the windfall had the potential to divide the church. Once word got around the congregation, there would be more ideas about how to spend the cash than people in the church.

As expected, some were angry I had given the directive to sell.

"We should have kept it in the stock market! You didn't operate within our bylaws."

I checked the bylaws. There was nothing in there about selling stock obtained through the demutualization process of an insurance provider.

Others wanted to add it to the building fund. For decades, the church had discussed building a family life center with a state-of-the-art gymnasium. Many felt we should add the cash to our reserve fund in case of a disaster. I was caught between many different viewpoints. In the middle of the debate was a big pile of cash.

This situation occurred many years ago when I was in my twenties. Perhaps what I decided to do was a product of my inexperience and lack of wisdom. Or maybe it was directed by the Holy Spirit. I still wonder. But I had a conviction about the direction the church needed to take.

The next Sunday, I stood in the pulpit and plainly told the church, "This money is not ours. It came to us by God's sovereignty, and it belongs to him. We're going to give it back to him. None of it will remain with the church. All of it will go to our missions partners."

We formed an ad hoc committee to determine the amounts to give to each missions partner, and over the course of several months every penny of the windfall went to support missions work all over the world. Amazingly, our reserve account ended up being fully funded that year. And my successor led the church through a capital campaign to build the family life center. That moment was a turning point for our church. If you want to grow locally, you must be willing to sacrifice everything for God's mission. You will never reach the neighborhood unless you also work to reach the nations.

The Neighborhood Church with a Global Mandate

Every local church has a global mandate. We share Jesus' truth and love with our neighbors. We share Jesus' truth and love with the nations. So much of *how* we pursue God's mission depends on our motivation. God's love is the compelling motivation of the neighborhood church. Paul told the Corinthians that Christ's love "controls" the church (2 Corinthians 5:14). The *"outward thrust"* of God's mission is derived from an *"inner compulsion"* of believers desiring to share Christ's love with those who do not know him.[1] A true movement of God's mission in the church is one that cannot be controlled; it spontaneously springs from the inner desire of believers.[2] The guiding force of this spontaneous movement is the textbook of missions, the Bible.[3] Christ's love compels the church outward. The Holy Spirit's activity is spontaneous and uncontrollable. And the guidebook to the nations is God's Word. When a neighborhood church becomes passionate for God's mission, it is both comforting and exhilarating. Comforting in that being within God's will brings unexplainable peace and unity. Exhilarating in that you will have no control over your next steps within God's will. A church on mission will be found at the ends of the earth with no map and no idea of what the next day will bring. You may find an extra $600,000 only to be told to give it all away.

A Stationary Church Is a Disobedient Church

The story of the Gospels is Jesus' movement *toward* Jerusalem, while the book of Acts tells the story of the church's movement *away* from Jerusalem. Jesus was determined to get to the Cross. Luke 9:51 records how Jesus "resolutely set out for Jerusalem." The original Greek literally translates "stiffened his face to go." The Cross was a divine necessity in the mission of God. Jesus was determined to get there. If Jesus' calling was into the Cross, then the church has a calling outward on God's mission to share about the Cross.

Acts 1:8 records the imperative from Jesus to his disciples: "You will be my witnesses." The directive to move is not optional. An inward-focused and stationary church is *always* disobedient. Where is the church to go? The imperative continues: "in Jerusalem, throughout Judea, in Samaria, and to the ends of the earth." Not only should every local church move outward, but every local church has a global mandate. The commands are not *consecutive*, as if we're to focus on the neighborhood first, and then as we have time and resources begin to move further outward to the ends of the earth. The commands are *parallel*, in that every local church should move toward the ends of the earth while also working to reach the neighborhood. Your church should be for the neighborhood *and* the nations *at the same time*.

Right after Jesus ascends to heaven in Acts 1, two angels appear to the disciples, who are understandably staring into the sky. The angels say, "Why are you standing here staring into heaven?" (Acts 1:11). Thus interpreted: "It's time to get moving!" As we learn from the priest and the Levite in the story of the Good Samaritan, resolving to do nothing is disobedience. An inactive Christian is a disobedient Christian. A stationary church is a disobedient church.

The Here and Hear of God's Mission

Most people feel uncomfortable in a place they don't know or around people who are different than they are. We can feel vulnerable, exposed, and less confident when we're somewhere unfamiliar or amidst a different culture. The problem is not that we might feel vulnerable in such situations. The problem is if we look at different people in different places and think, *I'm better. I'm more deserving.* Feeling uncomfortable and humbled can be a sign of being within God's will. If we feel discomfort while we are being obedient, it means we are moving outward on God's mission without a sense of entitlement.

A neighborhood church for the nations has two missiological motivations. The first is pursuing diversity *here*—drawing in all sorts of people from the neighborhood. The second is desiring that every people group would *hear* the gospel. The *here* and *hear* are quite important to the culture of the church. A healthy neighborhood church wants diversity within the congregation locally while also desiring to reach all nations globally.

Designed by God to Cross Every Boundary

One of my favorite family activities is overlanding. We load up my Toyota Land Cruiser and go to a remote place to hike, explore, and camp. My vehicle is designed to traverse long distances and handle off-road terrain. It gets the job done better than just about anything else on the road. The book of Romans refers to the feet of those who travel cross-culturally to share the gospel. Romans 10:15 specifically says, "How beautiful are the feet of messengers who bring good news!" Feet are not beautiful by most standards. What do feet do? Walk! What makes your feet attractive is not the physical features of ankles and toes, but whether they take you to someone who needs to hear about Jesus. The people of the church are the Land Cruisers of God's mission. We're supposed to load up and travel cross-culturally, often to places others would not go. Of course, we should grow in wisdom, discernment, and knowledge, but Scripture calls us to use our feet just as much as our minds.

When Jesus assembled the disciples at a mountain in Galilee right before his ascension, he gave them the Great Commission recorded in Matthew 28. Some scholars believe this mountain is the same one where the twelve were originally chosen. Imagine their emotions at this moment. They have been through so much leading up to this point. They have witnessed countless miracles by Jesus, including the resurrection of Lazarus, only to see Jesus die horrifically on the cross after they had all denied him and run away. Then they went from the low of the cross to the heights of Jesus' resurrection and appearances to them. Now they have gathered to hear Jesus' last words to them on earth. What does Jesus say?

> "I have been given all authority in heaven and on earth. Therefore, go and make disciples of all the nations, baptizing them in the name of the Father and the Son and the Holy Spirit. Teach these new disciples to obey all the commands I have given you. And be sure of this: I am with you always, even to the end of the age."
>
> MATTHEW 28:18-20

Jesus claims to have all the authority in the universe. He tells his disciples to go to all the nations. He promises to be with us always. The Great Commission contains five action verbs: *go*, *make*, *baptize*, *teach*, and *be sure*. *Go* implies crossing boundaries. We are to go across the street to our neighbors. We are to go cross-culturally. Go outside our comfort zones. Jesus assumes that the church will always go. Jesus gives a command, not a recommendation.

As the church goes, we are to *make* disciples. When we make something, we plan, shape, and form it. As believers, we're all works in progress, waiting for God to finish his good work in us (Philippians 1:6). None of us arrives spiritually on our own. We are a family of people in progress, working together as God shapes and forms us.

Most churches *baptize* in the name of the Father, Son, and Holy Spirit. "In the name of" suggests that our identity as believers is more than just a label. It's a calling. Our entire mission changes when we become disciples of Jesus. Why baptize in the *name* of the Father, Son, and Holy Spirit? The Father's love is given to us through his grace. The Son's sacrifice was made on our behalf. And the Holy Spirit's presence is with us, enabling us. The concept of the Trinity is essential to baptism. We do not baptize in the *names* (plural) but rather in the *name* (singular). God is one in three persons.

The command to *teach* is critical to God's mission. The structure in the text translates as "keep on teaching them." Faith in Christ is a lifelong process. We are saved in a moment in time, but we can always use more of the gospel every day. We should never stop growing. The goal of every believer is to take a deep dive into God's Word, teach what we learn to others, and learn from those who are more mature spiritually than we are.

The last action verb is to *be sure* or *remember*. God is with us through it all, until the end. He is there in the peaks and valleys.

God is there when we hear "congratulations" and when we hear "I'm sorry." He never leaves us. The problem is that many believers want the privileges of God's love without the responsibility to take God's love to the nations. We want the knowledge, the assurance, and the protection of salvation, but we struggle to share it with people in our neighborhoods and at the ends of the earth. Obedient Christians have active minds and active feet. We cannot grow spiritually without crossing cultural boundaries to share the message of Jesus. Stationary feet are ugly feet. But when our feet move with the gospel, they become beautiful in the eyes of God.

The language in Matthew 28 is also found in Matthew 24. The Great Commission and Matthew 24:14 refer to "nations" (*panta ta ethne* in Greek, meaning "all the nations"). This terminology alludes to something greater than geopolitical boundaries. It's even deeper than ethnolinguistic people groups. For Jesus' disciples, the Abrahamic covenant would come to mind.

Matthew 24:14 adds that Christ's return is pegged to our faithfulness in *going*:

> The Good News about the Kingdom will be preached throughout the whole world, so that all nations will hear it; and then the end will come.

Every neighborhood church also has a global mandate. The gospel *will* be preached to all people. The Good News *will* travel to every nation and tribe. If we care about the *end* of the story, we must do our part to *complete* the story. The church is the vehicle by which God's good news travels to the ends of the earth.

Conclusion

The Neighborhood
Church Returns

"Thanks for ruining my resignation letter," one pastor told us. His remark was tongue in cheek. Actually, he had contacted Church Answers to tell us the dramatic story of how his church had made a comeback.

"*God* ruined your resignation letter," I replied with a smile.

In many ways, his church fit all the stereotypes. Four white columns out front. A tall steeple hovering over a redbrick sanctuary with anchored down pews. This was a church with a regular weekly schedule and traditional programming. Sunday school at ten and worship at eleven. You could plant this church's building in just about any neighborhood of commensurate age, and it would fit right into the surroundings.

Inside the church, however, the temperature was rising. Tensions were building. A group of deacons met with the pastor to turn the pressure up a notch or two.

"You're ruining our church," they said bluntly.

These deacons were like a bullhorn constant blaring around the church. Most people in the congregation did not agree with them, but it was hard to ignore the commotion they created. Sometimes you can ignore your critics, and they'll disappear for lack of attention. But this group was bound and determined to bring things to a head.

The problem was much bigger than personal preferences within the church. The median age of the surrounding community was less than thirty years old. The demographics of the church were significantly older. Many in the congregation wanted to reach out to their Gen Z neighborhood, but the bullhorn deacons made any outreach difficult.

Dale had been the lead pastor for only a couple of years when everything started to blow up. The church had churned through a series of pastors before him. He was only in his mid-twenties, but the tension in the church was giving him more gray hairs every week.

He told us, "I remember thinking that I'm called here, but I'm going nowhere. The more I prayed, the hotter the fire got!"

When the date for his vacation arrived, he wondered if it was wise to leave, even for one week. Finally he decided to go, but he started writing his resignation letter during his time away. He also listened to the *Revitalize & Replant* podcast on ChurchAnswers .com, and that's where he heard cohost Mark Clifton say, "Get to year five before you quit!"

Dale knew he had not given the church enough time to transition. God convicted him to stay and work through the inevitable conflict that awaited his return.

Rather than writing a resignation letter, he wrote a sermon. It is now known as The Sermon among his congregants. A large crowd filled the sanctuary the Sunday he returned to the pulpit.

He laid out a vision for the congregation and rebuked those who were dividing the church. Over the course of eighteen unpleasant months, the antagonists left. The season was challenging, but the pruning was necessary.

"The Sunday after I laid it out there, we had four families visit our church. We never had guests before because most people in the community knew our reputation. But something had changed at that point. Every week, more guests kept coming."

After six membership classes and multiple people coming to Christ, the church is making a comeback. Nobody expected it—not those in the church and certainly not the community. It's a surprising return for a church everyone considered toxic. But these kinds of stories can multiply. I believe God is working among neighborhood churches.

"Love people even as your heart breaks for them," Dale said as our interview concluded. "Love people even when your anger boils because of them. When you brag about God, expect spiritual warfare. I was at my breaking point, and that's when God spoke to me most clearly."

Incredible potential is right around the corner. Imagine what could happen if neighborhood churches got healthy on a large scale. I believe the neighborhood church movement is primed for a relaunch.

Making the Comeback a Reality

Neighborhood churches tend to be small or midsize and well-established. For years, we have dismissed the potential for a significant move from God in these churches. They are numerous, and they are located in the heart of places with lots of people. I wish I could write that these churches *will* make a comeback, but it's still an unrealized possibility. But if such a comeback were to occur, what might it look like?

The Stigma Must Become the Advantage

Some have bemoaned the "on every street corner" nature of the established church. I understand. It seems there are churches everywhere that are doing nothing. But a shift is already underway. The megachurch movement is waning. The younger generations don't prefer the giant sanctuaries on sprawling campuses that their Boomer parents enjoyed. The neighborhood church has a long way to go before we can talk about a *movement*, but the stigma of *small and local* is fading. Smaller churches embedded in neighborhoods have a certain appeal. If these churches step up and begin to reach into their surrounding communities, that stigma might shift to an advantage.

Church Fostering Must Become More Common

We understand the term *fostering* in connection with children being placed with a family. It differs from adoption in that it's not intended to be permanent. Similarly, as we've already discussed, a new movement called fostering is emerging in the world of church revitalization, as relatively healthy churches provide people and other resources for relatively unhealthy churches over a specified time frame—usually six months to a year. In many cases, the fostering relationship involves sending in a preacher, improving the worship ministry, and restarting programming for children. The most successful fostering relationships also include outreach into the surrounding neighborhood.

Local Pastors Must Work Together for the Kingdom

In too many communities, pastors treat their church campuses like islands instead of as interconnected outposts in a Kingdom network. Pastors need to get off their islands and befriend other pastors. When pastors in a community become friends, tenures become longer and churches stop competing and start cooperating. The comeback of neighborhood churches will hit its stride when the pastors spend more energy working together than trying to compete.

Congregants Must Expect Growth and Invite Guests

Like Jupiter and Saturn compared to Mercury and Mars, larger churches have a greater gravitational pull than smaller churches. People who are new to a community or looking for a church are likely to visit the largest church in the area even if they don't anticipate joining. Larger churches will attract more guests. These churches expect to grow and anticipate having new people every Sunday.

Many, if not most, smaller, neighborhood churches do *not* have a culture or expectation of growth. And when you don't anticipate guests or invite people to church, it becomes a self-fulfilling prophecy. Many smaller churches remain small because the people there do not desire or expect growth. This entrenched mentality creates an unhealthy comfort with smallness and even ambivalence toward any new people who might upset the comfortable environment. When neighborhood churches make a comeback, it is often preceded by a cultural shift in the church—when the people start inviting others and expecting guests. If it's true, as we saw earlier, that 82 percent of the people in our neighborhoods are open to a personal invitation to attend church, "the fields are already ripe for harvest" (John 4:35).

Community Revitalization Must Become Part of the Mission

Revitalizing the church should include revitalizing the community. The way to better church health is through outward movement, not inward focus. Imagine a movement of neighborhood churches, each revitalizing a one-mile radius around their campuses. It would change the nation!

Selfless Service Must Replace Selfish Preferences

In Mark 10:35-40, when James and John ask Jesus to give them the highest places of honor in the Kingdom, he tells them they have no idea what they're asking. Greatness in God's Kingdom comes through sacrifice and service. How did Jesus serve? He gave his life! Selfish preferences are the death of selfless service. When you place your personal desires above another person's salvation, you are putting the mission of the church in great peril. Neighborhood churches will come back when the members elevate service above preference. A revitalized church will have more going and telling and less griping and yelling.

The Church Culture Bubble Must Pop

The insular church culture bubble will pop when your church pushes outward with the gospel. The church was never designed to be a shield protecting Christians from the world in a bubble of safety. The church is a vehicle engineered by God to take people into the darkest corners of the neighborhood. It's called the Great Commission, not the Great Avoidance. Gospel obedience compels us to go to the outcasts, the lowly, and the neglected. If you're not willing to sit down with a homeless addict and share the gospel because of how he or she looks and smells, then we don't believe the same gospel. Jesus doesn't call us to serve the most deserving, but he does call us to serve the most desperate.

The Campus Must Become a Neighborhood Hub

Church facilities are one of the most expensive, and yet vital, tools that church leaders use in shepherding God's people. In a North

American context, buildings are important to God's mission of expanding his Kingdom. Making the church building the locus of the community should be a priority for church leaders. From a practical standpoint, the church building should be the place where the local community congregates. Uninviting church buildings make it difficult for church members to invite their friends and family to worship with them.

It's time for the neighborhood church to make a comeback. The stigma of small churches is fading. Fostering is becoming more common. Pastors should feel free to leave the islands of their campuses and make friends. The opportunity to revitalize neighborhoods is as big as ever. The neighborhood church movement is primed for a relaunch.

The Impossible Becomes a Reality through the Miracle of Surrender

Reaching our neighbors requires that we surrender our time and convenience. Jesus understood what it was like to experience the unrelenting demands of serving people. In Mark 6:30-44, Jesus tries to escape the massive crowds after an exhausting day, retreating by boat to a quiet place with his disciples. But the crowds follow him on foot, beating him to the next destination. Instead of venting frustration and skirting off to another place, Jesus has deep compassion for the people.

Deciding that a meal is in order for everyone, he tells his disciples to feed the people. They calculate the cost of the meal and spin their heads over how to accomplish this task.

But the task is impossible. Jesus and the disciples are in the middle of the wilderness with more than 5,000 hungry people who are waiting to be fed both physically and spiritually. They don't have any money to purchase food; and even if they did, there's no place nearby to purchase it. All they can scrounge up are five small rolls and two dried fish.

Jesus looks up to heaven, appealing to God for the miraculous. The impossible becomes a reality through the power of God. Two dried fish and five rolls multiply. Kingdom resources don't run out. Everyone is satisfied. Even the poor have a full belly, maybe for the first time in their lives.

People from all different communities and backgrounds interact. Most of the surrounding towns had fewer than 3,000 people. A gathering of 5,000-plus would have been larger than most had ever seen. But the miracle of multiplying the food isn't the only important piece of the story. Perhaps just as important are the conversations that likely occurred after the meal. After eating together, small groups of people probably discussed the teaching they had received from Jesus.

The group was filled spiritually and physically. Yet as Jesus met their needs, he did so at the sacrifice of much-desired rest. Jesus surrendered time and convenience to reach a group of people searching for a sense of community.

Jesus Christ is the head of the body, the church. He shapes the community of the church and holds the members of the body together (Ephesians 4:15-16). When the body attempts to usurp the role of the head, things don't work the way they should. The essential connection of community must revolve around relationships focused on Christ. He is the bond and the glue. Changing the atmosphere of the church is not enough. Changing the church's setting or physical features won't solve the problem. The people of the church must make a conscious decision to stop looking inward and start reaching outward.

An inward church community is a dying community because they've lost their focus on the bond that holds them together. A vital church community will be centered on the person of Jesus Christ and the mission of spreading the message of salvation to everyone in the community outside the church. In other words, a healthy church community sacrifices its own needs and comfort to meet the needs of the community. Get people fired up about following Jesus and spreading the gospel and watch a strong church community emerge.

Do Everything You Can

At the height of his ministry, Jesus drew thousands of people to hear his teaching. He fed thousands of people with five loaves and two fish. In John 6:1-15, 22-58, Jesus is so popular that people attempt to take him by force and make him king. It is an odd scene until you realize the context. In the minds of the people, anyone who can miraculously produce free food is a good candidate for a position of authority.

What did they want? A free meal! How did Jesus respond? He says, in essence, "You don't need free bread. You need the Bread of Life."

But the people kept pushing him. They wanted a king who would give them free food. Jesus responds again.

"I tell you the truth, unless you eat the flesh of the Son of Man and drink his blood, you cannot have eternal life within you" (John 6:53). Jesus was speaking symbolically about his death on the cross, but the strong language caused the people to rethink his teaching.

Many of his disciples said, "This is very hard to understand. How can anyone accept it?" (John 6:60). At this point in Jesus' ministry, his popularity began to fall. Many people turned away.

Did they misunderstand Jesus? Was his teaching too cryptic? Did people start distancing themselves because Jesus did not make sense? Not at all.

The teaching was hard because people wanted something *from* Jesus. Many people were only interested in what Jesus could do for them. They were not interested in Jesus himself. How could they miss who Jesus was? It's not that they couldn't understand Jesus. It's that they were unwilling to accept him. Everyone loves free food Jesus. However, not everyone will choose to follow the flesh and blood Jesus.

In the church, the "free food" is all the things we get out of the services, events, and programs; but often we push back when it comes to making any real sacrifices. So what defines *your* level of commitment? Does your church meet your needs and fulfill your preferences? Or are you willing to give up all your preferences to accomplish God's mission in your neighborhood and around the world?

This book is about a collective movement of neighborhood churches, but I want to conclude with a personal challenge for *you*, the one reading or hearing these words right now. Are you doing everything you can to advance the mission of the church? Is there more you could do?

Our culture tends to believe we are free to do what we want, so long as we're not hurting anyone else. This idea has permeated our churches as well. If our preferences don't do any harm, they must be okay, right? Scripture teaches a different perspective.

Paul writes in 1 Corinthians 9:19 that our freedom in Christ should compel us to become slaves to others in order to bring them to Christ. The language is strong but necessary for the mission of the church. Christ frees us from sin. Then we make ourselves slaves to the message that freed us.

How do we make ourselves slaves? Paul offers an explanation in 1 Corinthians 9:22-23.

When I am with those who are weak, I share their
weakness, for I want to bring the weak to Christ. Yes,
I try to find common ground with everyone, doing
everything I can to save some. I do everything to spread
the Good News and share in its blessings.

Our goal is to do everything we can to find common ground
with others. Common ground enables us to share the good news
of Jesus in a gentle, respectful way (1 Peter 3:15-16). The idea is to
sacrifice our personal preferences without sacrificing God's truth.
Churches tend to be bastions of personal preferences. Even worse,
some will proclaim their preferences as if they are God's truth.

Many neighborhood churches are small. Many neighborhood
churches lack resources. But every church's best resource is the
power of Christ. We access this power through self-denial and
submission to the power of the Holy Spirit at work in our lives.
The gospel is worth it. It's worth giving up our preferences. It's
worth dying to ourselves to win others. The potential of a revitalized neighborhood church is worth everything we have.

Notes

Notes

CALLING FOR A COMEBACK

1. Baylor Religion Survey: Wave 5, *American Values, Mental Health, and Using Technology in the Age of Trump*, Baylor University, September 2017, 55, www.baylor.edu/baylorreligionsurvey/doc.php/292546.pdf.

2. Baylor Religion Survey, 56.

3. Outreach 100 is an annual list of the largest and fastest growing churches in the United States. It is published by *Outreach* magazine. https://outreach100.com.

4. The Hartford Institute for Religion Research does a regular survey on megachurches. In 2011, there were 1,611 churches averaging 2,000 or more in attendance. By early 2020 (pre-pandemic), there were around 1,750 churches averaging 1,800 or more in attendance. The reason for changing the threshold of a megachurch from 2,000 in attendance to 1,800 in attendance is unclear. Before the pandemic, the largest churches were still growing at the fastest rates. But there was not an increasing number of megachurches. How did the pandemic affect the largest churches? More research is needed. But the waning of the megachurch movement is occurring and had started prior to the pandemic.

5. Thom S. Rainer, *The Post-Quarantine Church* (Carol Stream, IL: Tyndale Momentum, 2020), 17.

6. The median church age is ninety-four years. See Cynthia Woolever and Deborah Bruce, *A Field Guide to U.S. Congregations: Who's Going Where and Why*, 2nd ed. (Louisville, KY: Westminster John Knox Press, 2010), 27.

7. The median church size in the United States is 75 people in attendance, but the median churchgoer attends a church of 400 people. See Mark Chaves, *American Religion: Contemporary Trends* (Princeton, NJ: Princeton University Press, 2011), 64.

YOUR ADDRESS IS YOUR ASSIGNMENT

1. Waveney Ann Moore, "Fewer parishioners, less money has Tampa Bay churches selling off property," *Tampa Bay Times*, June 14, 2019, https://www.tampabay.com/news/religion/fewer-parishioners-less-money-has-tampa-bay-churches-selling-off-property-20190617.
2. Francis M. DuBose, *God Who Sends: A Fresh Quest for Biblical Mission* (Nashville: Broadman Press, 1983), 60.
3. Clayborne Carson et al., eds., *The Papers of Martin Luther King, Jr., Volume VI: Advocate of the Social Gospel, September 1948–March 1963* (Berkeley: University of California Press, 2007), 482.
4. David Platt, *Radical: Taking Back Your Faith from the American Dream* (Colorado Springs: Multnomah, 2010), 156.
5. Robert G. Moss, *The Neighborhood Church: God's Vision of Success* (Eugene, OR: Wipf & Stock, 2014), 49-50.
6. See, for example, William Julius Wilson and Richard P. Taub, *There Goes the Neighborhood: Racial, Ethnic, and Class Tensions in Four Chicago Neighborhoods and Their Meaning for America* (New York: Vintage, 2007).
7. Diana Butler Bass, *Christianity for the Rest of Us: How the Neighborhood Church Is Transforming the Faith* (New York: Harper One, 2006), 15-25.
8. Thomas Maney, *Basic Communities: A Practical Guide for Renewing Neighborhood Churches* (Minneapolis: Winston Press, 1984), 23.

THE (BRIGHT) FUTURE OF NEIGHBORHOOD CHURCHES

1. Mary L. Ohmer et al., *Measures for Community and Neighborhood Research* (Los Angeles: SAGE Publications, 2019), 31-40.
2. James Howard Kunstler, *The Geography of Nowhere: The Rise and Decline of America's Man-Made Landscape* (New York: Touchstone, 1993), 147.
3. Lewis Mumford, *The City in History: Its Origins, Its Transformations, and Its Prospects* (San Diego: Harvest/Harcourt, 1961), 13.
4. Christopher Benfey, *If: The Untold Story of Kipling's American Years* (New York: Penguin Press, 2019), 156.
5. Timothy Keller, *Center Church: Doing Balanced, Gospel-Centered Ministry in Your City* (Grand Rapids: Zondervan, 2012), 135-143.
6. Keller, 135.
7. Andres Duany, Elizabeth Plater-Zyberk, and Jeff Speck, *Suburban Nation: The Rise of Sprawl and the Decline of the American Dream* (New York: North Point Press, 2000), 7-8.
8. Alan Ehrenhalt, *The Great Inversion and the Future of the American City* (New York: Alfred A. Knopf, 2012), 7, 208.
9. Arthur C. Nelson and Robert E. Lang, *Megapolitan America: A New Vision for Understanding America's Metropolitan Geography* (Chicago: Planners Press, 2011), 62-68.

10. Robert Bruegmann, *Sprawl: A Compact History* (Chicago: University of Chicago Press, 2005), 5.

11. Joel Kotkin, *The Next Hundred Million: America in 2050* (New York: Penguin Press, 2010), 146-148.

12. Dustin Willis and Brandon Clements, *The Simplest Way to Change the World: Biblical Hospitality as a Way of Life* (Chicago: Moody, 2017), 70.

13. Jason Young and Jonathan Malm, *The Come Back Effect: How Hospitality Can Compel Your Church's Guests to Return* (Grand Rapids: Baker Books, 2018), 88-89.

14. Jim Nostedt, "Monetizing Sustainability: The Total Cost of Building Ownership," (PowerPoint presentation, NS Ecology Action Centre, n.d.), https://ecologyaction.ca/sites/default/files/images-documents/issue_areas/NS%20Ecology%20Action%20Centre%20%20to%20SEEFAR%202020-08-19.pdf.

15. Wendell Cox, "Core City Population Losses Detailed," *New Geography*, May 29, 2022, http://www.newgeography.com/content/007462-core-city-population-losses-detailed.

16. Konrad Putzier, "Dreaded Commute to the City Is Keeping Offices Mostly Empty," *Wall Street Journal*, May 31, 2022, https://www.wsj.com/articles/dreaded-commute-to-the-city-is-keeping-offices-mostly-empty-11653989581.

17. Statistic from Scott Thumma's research on megachurches at Hartford Institute for Religion Research, as quoted in Jeff Brumley, "In a world of haves and have-nots, America's churches should capitalize on their strengths, religion researcher says," Baptist News Global, December 10, 2021, https://baptistnews.com/article/in-a-world-of-haves-and-have-nots-americas-churches-should-capitalize-on-their-strengths-religion-research-says/#.YkiIujMK3A.

18. Nicole Friedman, "Millennials Are Supercharging the Housing Market," *Wall Street Journal*, December 14, 2021.

19. Jade Scipioni, "Millennials have been moving out of big cities—here's where they are going," CNBC, April 15, 2021, https://www.cnbc.com/2021/04/15/millennials-moving-out-of-big-cities-where-they-are-going-smartasset.html.

20. This estimate uses an average household size of 2.6 in the United States.

THE MARKS OF A HEALTHY NEIGHBORHOOD CHURCH

1. Robert Lewis with Rob Wilkins, *The Church of Irresistible Influence: Bridge-Building Stories to Help Reach Your Community* (Grand Rapids: Zondervan, 2001), 28.

2. Tim Keller (@DailyKeller), Twitter, January 9, 2014, 6:31 a.m. https://twitter.com/dailykeller/status/421257802854592512.

3. Rick Rusaw and Brian Mavis, *The Neighboring Church: Getting Better at What Jesus Says Matters Most* (Nashville: Thomas Nelson, 2016), 4.

4. "Boyce Taylor Is Put In Jail At Murray," *Kentucky New Era*, April 18, 1919, 4, news.google.com/newspapers?nid=266&dat=19190418&id=f9srAAAAI BAJ&sjid=XEYEAAAAIBAJ&pg=4110,4402533.

5. Check out www.timboydcomedy.com.

6. Donald A. McGavran, *Understanding Church Growth*, rev. ed. (Grand Rapids, MI: Eerdmans, 1985). See chapter 2 in particular.

7. Jimmy Scroggins, "Built to Last." Southern Baptist Theological Seminary Chapel (2012), http://www.sbts.edu/media/video/chapel/spring-2012 /20120403-scroggins.mp4.

8. Paul Sparks, Tim Soerens, and Dwight J. Friesen, *The New Parish: How Neighborhood Churches Are Transforming Mission, Discipleship, and Community* (Downers Grove, IL: IVP, 2014), 121.

9. Krin Van Tatenhove and Rob Mueller, *Neighborhood Church: Transforming Your Congregation into a Powerhouse for Mission* (Louisville, KY: Westminster John Knox Press, 2019), 75.

A NEW FRAMEWORK TO UNDERSTAND NEIGHBORHOOD CHURCHES

1. Adapted from Sam Rainer, *The Church Revitalization Checklist: A Hopeful and Practical Guide for Leading Your Congregation to a Brighter Tomorrow* (Carol Stream, IL: Tyndale Momentum, 2021), 50-51.

2. Kara Bettis, "Surviving Spiritual Gentrification: When Neighborhoods Change, How Do Churches Know If They Still Belong?" *Christianity Today*, April 2022, vol. 66, no. 3, 42.

3. Hartford Institute for Religion Research (2021). Faith Communities Today Partnership Project, "Twenty Years of Congregational Change: The 2020 Faith Communities Today Overview."

MYTHS OF THE NEIGHBORHOOD CHURCH

1. Mark Chaves, *American Religion: Contemporary Trends* (Princeton, NJ: Princeton University Press, 2011), 65-66.

2. Tony Dale, Felicity Dale, and George Barna, *Small Is Big!: Unleashing the Big Impact of Intentionally Small Churches* (Carol Stream, IL: Barna, 2011), 157-164.

3. "Inflection Point," Corporate Finance Institute, April 7, 2021, https:// corporatefinanceinstitute.com/resources/knowledge/finance/inflection -point/.

4. Glenn C. Daman, *Shepherding the Small Church: A Leadership Guide for the Majority of Today's Churches*, 2nd edition (Grand Rapids, MI: Kregel, 2008), 43.

5. Brandon J. O'Brien, *The Strategically Small Church: Intimate, Nimble, Authentic, Effective* (Minneapolis: Bethany House, 2010), 14.

6. David R. Ray, *The Indispensable Guide for Smaller Churches* (Cleveland: Pilgrim Press, 2003), 92.

7. Anthony G. Pappas, ed., *Inside the Small Church* (Lanham, MD: Alban Institute, 2002), 151.

8. See, for example, *Turn Around Strategies for the Small Church* by Ron Crandall (Nashville: Abingdon Press, 1995).

9. Hannah Critchfield, "Gulfport church had 19 regular worshipers. Sunday's service was its last." *Tampa Bay Times*, April 26, 2022.

10. Critchfield.

11. Critchfield.

THE CURRENT CHALLENGES OF NEIGHBORHOOD CHURCHES

1. Carl F. George and Robert E. Logan, *Leading and Managing Your Church* (Old Tappan, NJ: Fleming H. Revell, 1988), 147-151.

2. In 2020, the birth rate in the United States was about 12 per 1,000 inhabitants while the death rate was about 9 per 1,000 inhabitants. See "Births, deaths and infant mortality," Institut National d'Etudes Démographiques (INED), https://www.ined.fr/en/everything_about_population/data/europe-developed-countries/birth-death-infant-mortality/.

3. If you're curious, you can view the paperwork the church filed, at this link: https://catalog.archives.gov/id/123848082.

4. Mark Clifton, *Reclaiming Glory: Revitalizing Dying Churches* (Nashville: B&H, 2016), 29.

5. Andrew M. Davis, *Revitalize: Biblical Keys to Helping Your Church Come Alive Again* (Grand Rapids, MI: Baker Books, 2017), 26.

6. Thom S. Rainer, *Autopsy of a Deceased Church: 12 Ways to Keep Yours Alive* (Nashville: B&H, 2014), 27-29.

7. Donald A. McGavran, *Understanding Church Growth*, 3rd edition (Grand Rapids, MI: Eerdmans, 1990), 163, 167.

8. Estimates are as high as 96 percent of growth in large churches is due to transfer growth. See Mike Breen, "Obituary for the American Church," *Mission Frontiers* (blog), July 1, 2012, www.missionfrontiers.org/issue/article/obituary-for-the-american-church.

9. Scott L. Thumma, "The Kingdom, the Power, and the Glory: Megachurches in Modern American Society" (PhD diss., Emory University, 1996), Hartford Institute for Religion Research, http://hirr.hartsem.edu/megachurch/dissertation.html.

10. See Warren Bird and Scott Thumma, "A New Decade of Megachurches: 2011 Profile of Large Attendance Churches in the United States," Leadership Network and Hartford Seminary (2011), Hartford Institute for Religion Research, http://www.hartfordinstitute.org/megachurch/megachurch-2011-summary-report.htm.

11. Aaron Earls, "The New Picture of American Megachurches," Lifeway Research, December 8, 2015, http://factsandtrends.net/2015/12/08/the-new-picture-of-americas-megachurches/#.WC811vkrLb0.
12. Earls.
13. Bob Smietana, "Willow Creek Cuts Staff Budget by $6.5 Million," *Christianity Today*, May 20, 2022, https://www.christianitytoday.com/news/2022/may/willow-creek-megachurch-staff-layoffs-covid-pandemic-attend.html.
14. Karl Vaters, *The Church Recovery Guide: How Your Congregation Can Adapt and Thrive after a Crisis* (Chicago: Moody, 2020), 32.

LEADING CHANGE IN THE NEIGHBORHOOD CHURCH

1. Lyle E. Schaller, *The Change Agent: The Strategy of Innovative Leadership* (Nashville: Abingdon, 1972), 46.
2. Ronald Reagan, "Remarks at a Reception for Members of the Associated General Contractors of America," March 16, 1981, Ronald Reagan Presidential Library and Museum, www.reaganlibrary.gov/archives/speech/remarks-reception-members-associated-general-contractors-america.
3. Aubrey Malphurs, *Pouring New Wine into Old Wineskins: How to Change a Church without Destroying It* (Grand Rapids, MI: Baker Books, 1996), 81-82.
4. Adapted from Sam Rainer, "Why the Status Quo Is So Tempting (and Dangerous)," *Church Answers* (blog), November 11, 2020, https://churchanswers.com/blog/why-the-status-quo-is-so-tempting-and-dangerous/.
5. Aubrey Malphurs, *Advanced Strategic Planning: A 21st-Century Model for Church and Ministry Leaders*, 3rd edition (Grand Rapids, MI: Baker Books, 2013).
6. Jim Herrington, Mike Bonem, and James H. Furr, *Leading Congregational Change: A Practical Guide for the Transformational Journey* (San Francisco: Jossey-Bass, 2000).
7. Bill Hull, *7 Steps to Transform Your Church* (Grand Rapids, MI: Fleming H. Revell, 1993), 19.

EFFECTIVE STRATEGIES TO REACH THE NEIGHBORS

1. "*Tsuga canadensis* (L.) Carr.: Eastern Hemlock," US Forest Service, Southern Research Station, accessed August 14, 2022, www.srs.fs.usda.gov/pubs/misc/ag_654/volume_1/tsuga/canadensis.htm.
2. Kim Parker and Juliana Menasce Horowitz, "Majority of workers who quit a job in 2021 cite low pay, no opportunities for advancement, feeling disrespected," Pew Research Center, March 9, 2022, www.pewresearch.org/fact-tank/2022/03/09/majority-of-workers-who-quit-a-job-in-2021-cite-low-pay-no-opportunities-for-advancement-feeling-disrespected.

3. Mark Chaves, *American Religion: Contemporary Trends* (Princeton, NJ: Princeton University Press, 2011), 68.
4. Thom S. Rainer and Sam S. Rainer III, *Essential Church?: Reclaiming a Generation of Dropouts* (Nashville: B&H, 2008), 95, 132.
5. John Fuder, *Neighborhood Mapping: How to Make Your Church Invaluable to the Community* (Chicago: Moody, 2014), 15, 39-42.
6. Lance Ford and Brad Brisco, *Next Door as It Is in Heaven: Living Out God's Kingdom in Your Neighborhood* (Colorado Springs: NavPress, 2016), 41.
7. Jay Pathak and Dave Runyon, *The Art of Neighboring: Building Genuine Relationships Right Outside Your Door* (Grand Rapids, MI: Baker Books, 2012), 45-46.
8. Tom Nelson, *The Economics of Neighborly Love: Investing in Your Community's Compassion and Capacity* (Downers Grove, IL: IVP, 2017), 17.
9. Thom S. Rainer, *The Unchurched Next Door: Understanding Faith Stages as Keys to Sharing Your Faith* (Grand Rapids: Zondervan, 2008), 24-25.
10. Bob Smietana, "Two-Thirds of Churchgoers Have Invited Someone to Church," Lifeway Research, July 12, 2018, https://research.lifeway.com/2018 /07/12/two-thirds-of-churchgoers-have-invited-someone-to-church.
11. For more information, see InviteYourOne.com.
12. Justin Nortey, "More houses of worship are returning to normal operations, but in-person attendance is unchanged since fall," Pew Research Center, March 22, 2022, https://www.pewresearch.org/fact-tank/2022/03/22/more -houses-of-worship-are-returning-to-normal-operations-but-in-person -attendance-is-unchanged-since-fall.

BECOMING A NEIGHBORHOOD CHURCH FOR THE NATIONS

1. Francis M. DuBose, *God Who Sends: A Fresh Quest for Biblical Mission* (Nashville: Broadman Press, 1983), 100.
2. Roland Allen, *The Spontaneous Expansion of the Church* (Eugene, OR: Wipf & Stock, 1962), 5, 7, 15.
3. William Owen Carver, *Missions in the Plan of the Ages: Bible Studies in Missions* (Nashville: Broadman Press, 1951), 20.

About the Author

Sam Rainer serves as president of Church Answers and is a cofounder of Rainer Publishing. He is also lead pastor at West Bradenton Baptist Church in Bradenton, Florida. He writes, teaches, speaks, and consults on a variety of church health issues. Sam cohosts the popular podcasts *Rainer on Leadership* and *EST.church*.

Sam is the author of *Obstacles in the Established Church*, *The Church Revitalization Checklist*, *Understanding the Bible as a Whole*, and the coauthor of *Essential Church?* He has written hundreds of articles for several publications and is a frequent conference speaker on church health issues.

Sam holds a BS in finance and marketing from the University of South Carolina, an MA in missiology from The Southern Baptist Theological Seminary, and a PhD in leadership studies from Dallas Baptist University. He lives in Bradenton with his wife and four children. The Rainers are also a foster family, so it's likely there are more kids in the house at any given time.

If you liked this book, you'll want to get involved in

Church Equip!

Do you have a desire to learn more about serving God through your local church?

Would you like to see how God can use you in new and exciting ways?

Get your church involved in Church Equip, an online ministry designed to prepare church leaders and church members to better serve God's mission and purpose.

Check us out at **ChurchEquip.com**